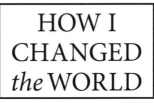

HOW I
CHANGED
the WORLD

Frederick Douglass

WORLD
BOOK

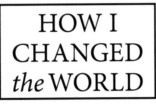

HOW I
CHANGED
the WORLD

Frederick
Douglass

WORLD
BOOK

World Book, Inc.
180 North LaSalle Street
Suite 900
Chicago, Illinois 60601
USA

For information about other "How I Changed the World" titles, as well as other World Book print and digital publications, please go to **www.worldbook.com**.

For information about other World Book publications, call 1-800-WORLDBK (967-5325).

For information about sales to schools and libraries, call 1-800-975-3250 (United States) or 1-800-837-5365 (Canada).

Library of Congress Cataloging-in-Publication Data for this volume has been applied for.

How I Changed the World
ISBN: 978-0-7166-2278-9 (set, hc.)

Frederick Douglass
ISBN: 978-0-7166-2280-2 (hc.)

Also available as:
ISBN: 978-0-7166-2286-4 (e-book)

Printed in China by Shenzhen Wing King Tong Paper Products Co., Ltd., Shenzhen, Guangdong
1st printing July 2018

CONTENTS

Born a Slave
7

From Slavery to Freedom
27

The Coming Civil War
51

The Struggle for Emancipation
67

Index
93

Further Reading/Acknowledgments
96

CHAPTER 1

Born a Slave

Family and Early Childhood

Frederick Douglass was a great African American statesman, abolitionist, social reformer, orator, and writer. He was born under the humblest of circumstances—he was born a slave. Despite his lowly upbringing, he rose to become a national leader in the movement to end slavery in the United States. Through his moving speeches and eloquent writings on the abolition of slavery, he was a role model for African Americans of his day. Frederick's life and work is a powerful reminder of the ongoing struggle for racial equality that continues today.

Frederick was born on a plantation near Tuckahoe Creek in Talbot County, Maryland, sometime in February of 1818. He was given the name Frederick Augustus Washington Bailey. The exact date of his birth is unknown, but he later chose to celebrate February 14 as his birthday, as his mother often called him "my valentine." Years later, after having escaped to the North, Frederick stopped using his two middle names and took the surname "Johnson." Eventually, he decided that Johnson was too commonplace and chose the last name by which he is now universally known.

Harriet Bailey, Frederick's mother, also was born a slave. While the identity of his father is unknown, Frederick knew his father was a white man. He grew up with the persistent rumor that his owner, Aaron Anthony, who was referred to as "Old Master," was his father. As an infant, Frederick was separated from his mother when she was sent to work on a farm about 12 miles away. Unfortunately, the separation of slave families, particularly mothers from their children, was not uncommon in the institution of slavery.

Harriet tried to see her son as much as she could, however. After a hard day's work as a field hand, she would sometimes return on foot at night to the small cabin where Frederick and his maternal grandparents, Betsey (called Betty) and Isaac, lived. Harriet would spend the night—and a few precious moments—with her son and then rise early the next day to return to the farm before dawn. She would retrace the steps of her 12-mile journey to avoid the punishment that

Frederick was born on a plantation near Tuckahoe Creek, Maryland, in 1818. Enslaved people were typically housed in cabins in slave quarters, similar to those shown below, on their owner's plantation.

When Frederick was a small boy, he lived on Edward Lloyd's plantation. This is the Wye House mansion, from which Lloyd oversaw his vast property and over 1,000 enslaved people.

would come with being late to work. Sadly, Harriet died of an unknown illness when Frederick was a small boy. Afterward, his grandmother raised him. Frederick dearly loved his "Grandmother Betty," as she was known among the family. She was renowned for her fishing and gardening skills.

The Knowledge of Being Enslaved

Under the care of his loving grandmother, Frederick had fond, simple memories of his early childhood. However, as he grew older, he gradually became aware of the dark shadow of slavery that hung over the life of his family. More and more, he would hear his grandparents speak in hushed tones about Old Master. In time, Frederick learned that the cabin in which he lived, along with the surrounding woodland, belonged to this person. Eventually, he came to understand that his grandparents, his cousins, and even he himself were considered the property of Old Master.

Around the age of 7, Frederick was taken away from his grandmother—and the life he had known—and moved to a plantation on Wye Island in rural Talbot County. Frederick was brokenhearted. Though Frederick found himself in the company of his siblings and older cousins, the sorrow caused by the loss of his grandmother remained with Frederick until the end of his life.

Eventually, he came to understand that his grandparents, his cousins, and even he himself were considered the property of Old Master.

The plantation where Frederick now lived was owned by Colonel Edward Lloyd, who oversaw his vast property from a mansion known as "Wye House." One of the most prosperous plantations in all of Maryland, it was so large that more than a thousand enslaved people were required to maintain it. Frederick's owner, Aaron Anthony, was the chief overseer of the plantation. He was known as the "Captain" because of the time he spent sailing on Chesapeake Bay. Anthony himself owned three farms near the Tuckahoe. Because Frederick was so young, he was not yet required to do heavy work. However, most of the slaves who lived under Captain Anthony's watch suffered brutal conditions. Every day Frederick spent there, he saw his fellow slaves being beaten and cruelly treated.

Captain Anthony had two sons, Andrew and Richard, and one daughter, named Lucretia. Lucretia often showed kindness to Frederick by giving him food and caring for him in other ways. By the time Frederick was aware of the family that owned him, Lucretia had married a man named Thomas Auld. When Frederick was around 8 years old, Captain Anthony fell ill and was removed from his post as the overseer of the Wye House plantation. He returned to one of his farms, taking his family and the slaves that he owned with him. Recognizing that Frederick was a remarkable child and not wanting to abandon him to the life of a field hand, Lucretia and her husband arranged to have him serve under Thomas's brother, Hugh, in Baltimore. This news overjoyed young Frederick, who was looking forward to the possibility of a new and better life.

Life in Baltimore

Hugh Auld and his wife, Sophia, lived in Fells Point, a busy shipbuilding center on the east side of Baltimore's harbor. When Frederick arrived there, he was met by his new mistress. "Miss Sophia," as Frederick would call her, smiled at him with the "most kindly emotions." He had never encountered white people who treated him so well. On the plantation, he had been treated little better than an animal. In Baltimore, Frederick was treated kindly.

Frederick's new home was warm and inviting, and he was happy with the changes in his life. The rough shirt he had been given on the plantation—his only piece of clothing—was replaced with pants and a

13

new shirt he could tuck inside his pants. Instead of sleeping in a grain sack on cold nights, Frederick now had a straw bed with covers. Hugh and Sophia also had a child of their own, a 2-year-old boy named Tommy. It became Frederick's task to look after Tommy. As a devoted Methodist, Miss Sophia would often sit with her son on one knee and the Bible on the other, drawing Frederick to her side and telling stories to both boys.

Shortly after his arrival in the Auld family home, Miss Sophia began to teach Frederick to read. Although these lessons started innocently enough, they would prove to be a turning point in Frederick's life. They signaled the beginning of the end of Frederick's slavery and would slowly but surely shape him into the great leader he was to become. From that moment on, Frederick remained aware of the power that came with knowing how to read and write. Later in life, he would refer to it as "the pathway from slavery to freedom."

> *. . . Frederick remained aware of the power that came with knowing how to read and write.*

Then one day Sophia showed her husband what Frederick had learned. Hugh Auld was not pleased, however, and insisted that the lessons stop at once. He recognized Frederick's intellectual promise and understood, even if his wife did not, the dangerous pursuit in which she was engaged. One reason for his displeasure was that it was against the law to teach a slave to read. Another reason was because learning could make slaves unhappy and unmanageable.

Frederick would later describe the lecture that Hugh Auld gave his wife as the first "decidedly antislavery" speech he ever heard. Auld's lecture emphasized slavery's basic injustice. Ever since his time at Wye House, Frederick had known that slavery was bad and something that should be ended. That belief had now become fully articulated for him.

Many abolitionists distributed pamphlets on ways to end slavery.

Forbidden to read in the Auld family home, Frederick nevertheless continued his lessons in secret from white children in the neighborhood and from men who worked in the shipyards. When he was left alone, he would retrieve Tommy's copybook and write down the words he had learned to spell. Around the age of 12, he discovered *The Columbian Orator,* a book first published in 1797 for use in the classroom. In it, Frederick read essays and speeches that helped define his views on freedom and human rights. Then one day he found a newspaper and read an article about petitions in Congress "praying for the abolition of slavery." Suddenly he had learned a new word: abolition. It was one that would stay with him for the rest of his life.

James Madison

A PLAN

FOR

THE GRADUAL

ABOLITION OF SLAVERY

IN THE

UNITED STATES,

WITHOUT DANGER OR LOSS

TO THE

CITIZENS OF THE SOUTH.

———

BALTIMORE:
PRINTED BY BENJAMIN LUNDY—CAMDEN STREET.

1825.

The "Slave Breaker"

Frederick experienced a good deal of upheaval in Baltimore. During those years, a series of deaths occurred in Captain Anthony's family, including the Captain himself and his daughter, Lucretia. When this happened, the ownership of the Captain's property—including his slaves—changed hands. As he was considered part of that property, Frederick was sent back to the plantation for the reading of Captain Anthony's last will and testament. This, of course, caused a great deal of distress for Frederick. Around the time he was 15 years old, Frederick was put on a boat and sent to the rundown port city of St. Michaels, Maryland, and his new master, Thomas Auld, Lucretia's husband.

Upon his arrival in St. Michaels, Frederick's new master decided that life in Baltimore had spoiled him and sent him to work for a man in the region named Edward Covey. Covey was a poor farmer who had the reputation of breaking the spirit of young slaves. He was known as a "slave breaker." For the first time in his life, Frederick found himself working in the fields. One cold morning, Frederick was sent into the woods with a team of oxen. Having no real experience with farm ani-

COLUMBIAN ORATOR:

CONTAINING

A VARIETY OF

ORIGINAL AND SELECTED PIECES,

TOGETHER WITH

R U L E S;

CALCULATED TO IMPROVE YOUTH AND OTHERS IN THE
ORNAMENTAL AND USEFUL

ART OF ELOQUENCE.

BY CALEB BINGHAM, A. M.
Author of the American Preceptor, Young Lady's Accidence, &c.

"Cato cultivated Eloquence as a necessary mean for defending the Rights of
the People, and for enforcing good Counsels."—Rollin.

Stereotype Edition.

Published in Boston,

BY J. H. A. FROST, LINCOLN AND EDMANDS, STIMPSON AND CLAPP,
MARSH, CAPEN AND LYON: NEW-YORK, COLLINS AND HANNAY:
TROY, N. Y., WILLIAM S. PARKER: PHILADELPHIA, GRIGG
AND ELLIOT: BALTIMORE, CUSHING AND SONS:
CINCINNATI, HUBBARD AND EDMANDS.

1832.

mals, Frederick lost control of them. To punish Frederick, Covey beat him savagely.

For the next six months, regular work—plowing and tending the fields—and regular beatings continued for Frederick. Because of this inhumane treatment, Frederick decided to run away, returning on foot to St. Michaels. By the time he arrived on the doorstep of Thomas Auld's home, Frederick's clothes were torn and muddied. When Frederick informed his master of the way he was being treated and asked for help, he received none and was immediately sent back to Covey's farm.

Then one day in the summer of 1834, after numerous beatings at Covey's hands, Frederick finally decided to fight back. In fact, he fought both Covey and one of his cousins. Being stronger than either man, Frederick won the fight. Most surprisingly, he was not beaten for it, and Covey never beat Frederick again. This proved to be another turning point in Frederick's life. He saw himself as a man now and was determined to be a free man.

The Freeland Farm

Frederick spent the Christmas of 1834 in St. Michaels at the Auld family home. The week between Christmas and New Year's Day was a time of rest and celebration, and slaves were usually relieved of most of their work during that time. In January, Frederick was sent to work on another farm. This time, Thomas Auld hired him out to a man named William Freeland for the entire year of 1835. Compared to Edward Covey, Freeland was a lenient master.

While Frederick worked on the Freeland farm, he taught the other slaves who lived there to read the Bible. Word spread about Frederick's Sunday school, and interest among his fellow slaves grew to the point that, in any given week, more than 40 people would attend the classes. Freeland generally ignored their study for several months. However, other white owners of nearby plantations were angered when they learned that their slaves were being taught to read and write. One Sunday morning, some of the slaveholders disrupted Frederick's classes and put an end to them permanently. Shortly afterward, Frederick and some of his friends began making plans to escape the bonds of slavery once and for all.

He saw himself as a man now and was determined to be a free man.

The night before their intended escape, Frederick found himself unable to sleep. He was afraid of being caught or killed, or perhaps sold to someone in the Deep South where slaves were treated with even greater cruelty than in Maryland. Frederick and his friends weighed their options. They knew there was no slavery in nearby Pennsylvania, just on the other side of the Mason-Dixon Line. This east-west boundary between Maryland and Pennsylvania and part of West Virginia was considered the dividing line between slave states and free states where slavery was banned. There was also no slavery in New York City, but it had a bad reputation of returning runaway slaves to their masters. Finally, there was distant Canada, with its promise of freedom. Since all these places lay to the north, Frederick and his friends thought it would be best to begin their journey by heading up the Chesapeake. Unfortunately, Frederick and his friends would never get that far. Although it remains uncertain, one of Frederick's companions who backed out at the last minute apparently had betrayed Frederick and the others by informing Freeland of their plans.

That morning, Frederick began his chores as usual. Then suddenly the sheriff and a small posse of heavily armed men on horseback arrived on the Freeland farm and rounded up the slaves they suspected of attempting to escape. The sheriff gave the order for Frederick and his friends to be brought into town. They were tied up and dragged behind the horses, stumbling all 15 miles until they reached the Talbot County jail. Once there, many white people called for them to be hanged. Fortunately for Frederick and his friends, however, the authorities had no proof of their escape plans and they were returned to their owners.

Nevertheless, Frederick had been identified as the ringleader of the plot. Several slaveholders near the Freeland farm threated to hang Frederick if he remained in the vicinity. Recognizing the danger, Frederick's master, Thomas Auld, decided to return him to his brother, Hugh, in Baltimore.

Anna Murray

Back in Baltimore, Frederick was hired out to one of the city's shipyards and learned the trade of caulking boats, that is, making them watertight. A quick

Anna Murray was among the free African Americans Frederick met while enslaved in Baltimore. The two quickly fell in love and eventually were married. With Anna's help, Frederick was able to escape to the North—and freedom.

learner, Frederick became an expert caulker within a year. Eventually, Hugh Auld allowed Frederick to hire himself out and make some extra money, with the condition that he could pay his master every Saturday evening for the "privilege" of being able to work independently. Frederick was forced to turn over his earnings whether he had work or not. Though he remained a slave, Frederick felt that being able to hire himself out would aid in his ability to escape from slavery.

During this time, Frederick also developed friendships with many young, free African Americans living in Baltimore. Some of them belonged to a debate club called the East Baltimore Mental Improvement Society. In 1837, Frederick joined the group and took part in some stirring debates. This was the beginning of his career as a great orator.

One of the people Frederick met during this time was a young woman named Anna Murray. She was among the free African Americans of Baltimore who welcomed Frederick into their group. Anna worked as a housekeeper for a family named Wells. She was hard-working and independent and about five years older than Frederick. Although illiterate, Anna was a powerful woman who would change the course of Frederick's life. Her status as a free African American woman reinforced Frederick's belief in the possibility of one day gaining his own freedom. The two of them quickly fell in love and began talking about how to achieve that goal.

One Saturday in the summer of 1838, Frederick made plans with some friends to attend a church meeting where debates about slavery were often held. It was at meetings like these that Frederick heard preachers speak about a loving God who created all people to be equal, and he decided to become a Christian. That evening, however, Frederick was kept working at the shipyard later than usual, and the church meeting was being held about 12 miles outside of Baltimore. Frederick knew that he would not

> *Anna was a powerful woman who would change the course of Frederick's life.*

have time to go to Hugh Auld's house to pay him for the week and then attend the meeting, so he decided to pay the money to his master after he got back. When he returned home that night, Hugh Auld, afraid that Frederick had escaped, was furious. He punished Frederick by no longer allowing him to hire out his own time to make extra money. This effectively ended any hope Frederick had to gain his freedom. Still, he knew he had to at least try to escape—before it was too late. With Anna's help, he arranged to do so.

Escape to the North

The date Frederick and Anna chose for his escape to the North—and freedom—was September 3, 1838. It took them three weeks to lay the groundwork for their journey. It was a time of great tension and busy preparation. The plan was for Frederick to make his way to New York City. After his arrival there, he would send for Anna. Once the two of them stood on the soil of a free state, they would be married. Before any of that could happen, however, they would need to buy tickets for carriages, trains, ferries, and steamships. Frederick had been able to save about six dollars a week after paying what he owed to Hugh Auld, and with her job as a domestic servant, Anna had put some money aside. She also sold a featherbed to help finance the trip. Between the two of them, they had saved enough for their dangerous venture.

In those days, when free African Americans traveled, the state of Maryland required them to carry papers that proved that they weren't slaves. Anna came up with the idea for Frederick to impersonate a sailor. She knew their plan would not work if Frederick wore shabby clothing and simply tried to blend in, something he was never very good at. With her skills as a seamstress, Anna altered his clothes to make him look the part. Frederick wore a red shirt with a kerchief loosely tied around his neck and a sailor's flat-topped, wide-brimmed hat. He had managed to obtain the necessary papers to travel from an acquaintance who was a free sailor. With his so-called "free papers" in hand, Frederick made his way to the train station.

Upon his arrival, Frederick bypassed the ticket window by waiting outside until just before the train was supposed to pull out. By doing so, Frederick avoided standing in line where the ticket master would have asked to see his papers and discovered that they did not match the passenger's description. With his

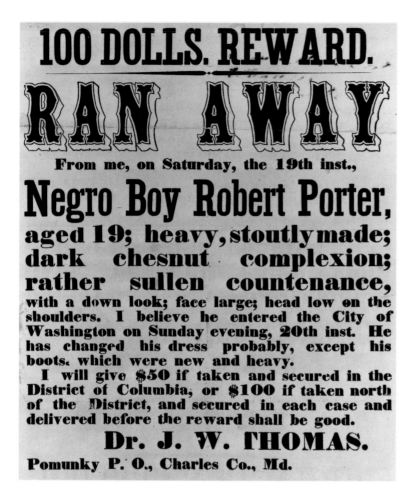

100 DOLLS. REWARD.

RAN AWAY

From me, on Saturday, the 19th inst.,

Negro Boy Robert Porter,

aged 19; heavy, stoutly made; dark chesnut complexion; rather sullen countenance, with a down look; face large; head low on the shoulders. I believe he entered the City of Washington on Sunday evening, 20th inst. He has changed his dress probably, except his boots, which were new and heavy.

I will give $50 if taken and secured in the District of Columbia, or $100 if taken north of the District, and secured in each case and delivered before the reward shall be good.

Dr. J. W. THOMAS.

Pomunky P. O., Charles Co., Md.

During his escape to the North, Frederick was faced with the threat of discovery at every turn. Slave traders were always on the lookout for runaway slaves. This is a reward notice for a runaway slave in Maryland in the late 1850's.

bag in hand, Frederick jumped on the train at the last minute and was on his way to Wilmington, Delaware—the first stop on his way to freedom.

The train moved swiftly, and the car that Frederick had boarded was full of people. Frederick began to worry as he watched the conductor's less-than-friendly encounters with the other black passengers. When the conductor reached Frederick, he saw that Frederick was dressed as a sailor and asked, "I suppose you have your free papers with you?" Calling upon all his courage, Frederick spoke in a calm voice. "No, sir," he said, "I never carry my free papers to sea with me." Frederick pulled out his borrowed seaman papers and showed them to the conductor, who most likely focused on the proud American eagle at the top rather than the description of the man who carried them. Taking Frederick's money, he quickly moved on to the next passenger. Frederick breathed a sigh of relief. He knew he had just overcome his first major obstacle.

The next day, Frederick was faced with the threat of discovery at every turn. Upon reaching Wilmington—and the most dangerous part of his journey—he stepped off the train and boarded a steamboat. He was nearing the border between the slave states and

Upon his arrival in New York, Frederick met a member of the underground railroad. This secret network helped countless runaway slaves escape from the South to the free Northern States and Canada.

the free states. Wilmington was always full of slave traders on the lookout for enslaved men and women attempting to flee north to gain their freedom. However, no one bothered Frederick, and he was soon on the "broad and beautiful" Delaware River, speeding toward the "Quaker City" of Philadelphia. The city had become a center of the antislavery movement.

When Frederick stepped onto Philadelphia's docks, he was a free man. He experienced a peace he had never known before. At the same time, he knew his journey was far from over, and he had no time to waste. He stopped a fellow African American and asked him the best way to get to New York City. The man pointed him in the right direction. Minutes later, Frederick boarded a ferry for the next leg of the trip. He then caught the overnight train and a final ferry to New York. Once he reached his destination, Frederick found himself both relieved and excited. His high spirits did not last long, however, as it dawned on him that he was now a fugitive from the law. He could be recaptured and sent back to Maryland—and slavery— at any moment.

Afraid to ask for directions, Frederick walked the streets of New York for several days. He did his best to deal with his feelings of isolation and loneliness. At night, he would sleep in alleyways or by the docks. Then Frederick stumbled upon a sailor, whose name was Stuart, and risked everything by telling him his story. Stuart responded by taking Frederick to his home for the night. The following day, as any friend of a runaway slave would do, Stuart walked with Frederick to the house of a kind man named David Ruggles.

Dedicated to the abolition of slavery, Ruggles was a member of the New York Vigilance Committee. The committee was a group of men and women who helped fugitive slaves through a system known as the underground railroad. This was a network of secret routes and safe houses established by abolitionists to help slaves escape from the South to the free Northern States and Canada. The underground railroad provided food, clothing, and shelter for the countless runaways who were pouring into New York. The underground railroad also helped the runaways reach places of safety. Ruggles welcomed Frederick into his home, allowing him to complete his plan of escape. It was then that Frederick Bailey chose "Johnson" as his new surname and wrote to Anna to join him in New York City. Anna arrived there shortly afterward without incident. On September 15, 1838, in the presence of David Ruggles and two or three other witnesses, Frederick and Anna were married. Anna was dressed in a plum-colored silk dress, and Frederick wore the good suit he had taken with him in his sailor's bag. The ceremony was performed by James W. C. Pennington, another fugitive from Maryland, who was just beginning his career as a Presbyterian minister and an advocate of African American equality. Immediately after the wedding, Frederick and Anna set off for New England and a new life together.

The underground railroad provided food, clothing, and shelter for the countless runaways who were pouring into New York.

CHAPTER 2

From Slavery to Freedom

A New Life

David Ruggles recommended that Frederick and Anna move to New Bedford, Massachusetts. When he learned that Frederick had experience with caulking boats, he was sure that there would be plenty of work for Frederick there. Another reason was that he knew a man there named Nathan Johnson. Nathan and his wife, Mary (also known as Polly), were members of the underground railroad. When Frederick and Anna arrived at the Johnson home, the newlyweds were overwhelmed by the couple's kindness and generosity. The Johnsons helped them, as Frederick would later say, "in the hour of my extremest need."

Shortly after arriving in New Bedford, Nathan suggested that Frederick change his last name. He thought a new name was in order, in part, because Johnson was such a common name in New Bedford. Aware that Frederick had a fondness for literature, Nathan looked to the famous poem, *The Lady of the Lake* (1810), by Sir Walter Scott. One of the poem's heroic characters is called James Douglas. Frederick liked the sound of the name and took it as his own, choosing the usual spelling of "Douglass" at the time.

As David Ruggles had hoped, Frederick was able to find work in New Bedford. However, although Massachusetts was a free state, prejudice remained a part of Frederick's life. Threatened by white workers if he took the well-paying job of being a caulker, Frederick was forced to take any job he could find. He shoveled coal, swept chimneys, and loaded and unloaded ships on the wharves. Around this time, Frederick and Anna also started a family. Their first child, a

daughter named Rosetta, was born on June 24, 1839. Sixteen months later, on October 9, 1840, Anna gave birth to a son named Lewis Henry. They would have five children in all—Frederick Junior, born March 3, 1842; Charles Remond, born October 21, 1844; and Annie, born March 22, 1849. Although the young family did not have much money and continued to face challenges, it was overall a happy time.

Frederick and Anna settled into the African American community in New Bedford and looked for a church where they could worship. Firmly believing in the equality of men and women, Frederick and his wife attended the Elm Street Methodist Church, a mostly white congregation. When they first arrived, they were directed to an upstairs gallery where other African American members of the church were seated. They were disappointed when they realized the church practiced segregation (the act of separating

Settling in New Bedford, Massachussets, Frederick remained aware that, although Massachusetts was a free state, he was still a fugitive slave. This is a view of neighboring Fairhaven from New Bedford's shores.

blacks from whites). After visiting several other churches in New Bedford, Frederick and Anna joined the African Methodist Episcopal Zion Church (A.M.E. Zion). The church had been founded in New York City in 1821 and was a leader in the antislavery movement. It counted among its members the famous abolitionists Harriet Tubman and Sojourner Truth.

Preacher and Abolitionist

At A.M.E. Zion Church, Frederick met Bishop Christopher Rush, who encouraged him to take on a leadership role in the community. Frederick established himself as a lay preacher and began giving sermons to the congregation. It was his first experience as a public speaker. Soon Frederick and Anna had prominent positions in the relative safety of the African American community of New Bedford. They moved into a larger house as their family grew. Before long, however, Frederick longed for something more than simple respectability. He was troubled by the fact that many of his fellow churchgoers did not wish to discuss the topic of antislavery because it was too controversial. Frederick himself was torn. On the one hand, he was eager to put his past as an enslaved person behind him. But on the other, he recognized that slavery was part of his story—and it was one that he wanted to tell.

About five months after moving to New Bedford, Frederick came one step closer to his true calling in life. He became aware of a newspaper called *The Liberator,* edited by the famous abolitionist William Lloyd Garrison. Garrison had become convinced of the need to end slavery and published the first issue of *The*

Liberator on January 1, 1831. In it, he argued strongly against the injustice and oppression of slavery. In time, Garrison effectively became the leader of the abolition movement. He was also instrumental in founding the Massachusetts Anti-Slavery Society and American Anti-Slavery Society. Although Frederick did not have much spare time as a father and working man, he made a point of reading *The Liberator* from cover to cover. It was a newspaper after his own heart. For the first time in his life, Frederick truly understood what it meant to be an abolitionist. He also became aware of the movement that was sweeping the United States, as well as Great Britain. There was a growing number of people who wanted to end slavery, and their voices

Fugitive slave laws were laws that provided for the return to their owners of runaway slaves who escaped to another state. Free blacks in the North were sometimes kidnapped and taken South as slaves.

PRACTICAL ILLUSTRATION OF THE FUGITIVE SLAVE LAW.

were becoming a powerful chorus. Frederick decided he wanted to be part of it.

At a meeting at Zion Church, the topic of colonization was debated. The meeting took place on March 12, 1839. That night, Frederick gave a powerful speech that harshly criticized the idea of sending slaves back to Africa. He told the audience how he believed that all slaves should be set free to live their lives in America. Making the speech was a memorable experience for Frederick, and reading about it in *The Liberator* days later was thrilling. This was another first for Frederick. The world had taken note of him. He was asked to speak again at another meeting. Primarily a white audience who held antislavery views attended this meeting. In a moving address, he related his personal experiences as a slave.

He told the audience how he believed that all slaves should be set free to live their lives in America.

The following month, Frederick attended a speech given by Garrison himself, one of the most famous abolitionists in America at the time. Speaking before an integrated audience, Garrison proved to be a charismatic orator. He was determined to end slavery in America and called for the "immediate emancipation" of all men and women in bondage. Through this speech, Frederick was "brought in contact with the mind of William Lloyd Garrison." He saw in Garrison what he wanted to become. From that moment on, he was no longer interested in being "a local preacher." Instead, he intended to wage his battle against slavery on a wider front.

In the spring of 1841, Frederick once again spoke against the practice of slavery at an antislavery meeting at Zion Church. He described to his neighbors what life as a slave had been like for him. In the congregation that evening was a man named William Coffin. Coffin was a white bookkeeper in the Merchants Bank, a Quaker, and a dedicated abolitionist. He was impressed with Frederick's persuasive words and thought that more people should hear what Frederick had to say. Coffin spoke with him after the meeting. He told Frederick about a large antislavery convention that was to take place that summer in Nantucket, a nearby island off the shore of New Bedford. After listening to Coffin, Frederick decided that he should attend.

Frederick referred to his visit to Nantucket as his "holiday." Since his escape from slavery three years earlier, he had worked hard to support his wife, Anna, and his two infant children. He had taken no time to rest. Now he would do so, but this visit would also have a purpose. Coffin not only wanted Frederick to attend the antislavery convention, but he also wanted him to speak. At first, Frederick was surprised by the offer. It was almost unheard of for a fugitive slave to address a mostly white audience. When Frederick finally agreed to do so, he was filled with excitement.

Frederick's address to the Nantucket Anti-Slavery Convention took place on August 16, 1841. He was only 23 years old, and it was a moment of great importance and emotion for him. When he stepped onto the speakers' platform, everyone in the audience was looking at him. Initially, Frederick's nervousness got

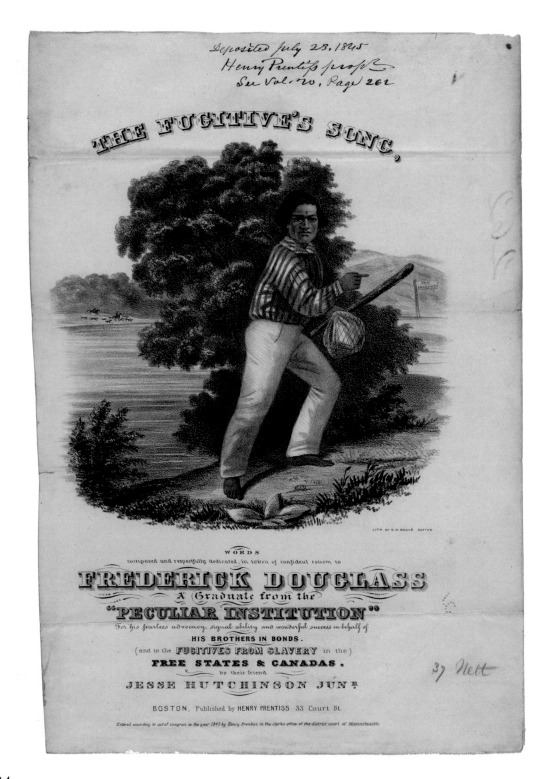

the better of him. He spoke haltingly and seemed distracted. Then everything that he had taught himself by reading *The Columbian Orator* came back to him, and he began to tell his story. More important, he was telling his story and people were listening to it! Most of them were white people he had never met before, and many of them were important people. Frederick was not the first former slave to speak to such an audience, but that night on Nantucket it was clear to everyone that a powerful new voice in the abolition movement had just been heard.

After Frederick gave his inspiring address, he was approached by a man named John Collins. A member of the Massachusetts Anti-Slavery Society, Collins invited Frederick to join the organization as a speaker. At first, Frederick wasn't interested. He did not see how he would be able to support his family if he spoke at antislavery conventions. There was also the fact that Frederick was still a slave in the eyes of the law. His master, Thomas Auld, was still pursuing him. If he became a public speaker, slave hunters in the North might learn about him, capture him, and return him to a life of slavery. Collins, however, was persuasive and finally convinced Frederick to go with him on a three-month tour.

A New Career

The three months that Frederick agreed to tour with Collins quickly turned into a new career for Frederick. He soon became thrilled at the prospect of serving as an agent of the Massachusetts Anti-Slavery Society. Before embarking on this new venture, how-

"The Fugitive's Song" is an abolitionist song that was composed in honor of Frederick Douglass, who had escaped from slavery. This image shows Frederick as a runaway slave on a sheet music cover.

ever, Frederick moved his family, which had just begun to plant its roots in New Bedford. Shortly after settling in Lynn, Massachusetts, he began his whirlwind tour. Collins and other well-known abolitionists often accompanied him. Frederick spoke passionately against slavery in many cities and towns in the North. At the same time, he continued to face discrimination.

Garrison held Frederick in high regard and would often publish Frederick's articles in his newspaper, The Liberator.

One time when he was traveling with Collins, the two of them intended to sit together during the train ride to an antislavery meeting in Dover, New Hampshire. When the conductor came along, he told Frederick to go to the "negro car." Frederick refused. The conductor then called upon several men to remove him by force. This happened to Frederick more than once, and he fought hard to end the practice of segregation on the Eastern Railroad. During this period, Frederick also began to spend a lot of time with William Lloyd Garrison and came to know him on a personal level. Garrison became Frederick's mentor, and Frederick embraced Garrison's philosophy of life, including his views on slavery, women's rights, and the practice of nonviolence. In turn, Garrison held Frederick in high regard and would often publish Frederick's articles in his newspaper, *The Liberator*. The publication assisted young Frederick's rise to national prominence.

As he continued his speaking tour with the Massachusetts Anti-Slavery Society, Frederick amazed his audiences with his strong voice and powerful message.

He shared with them the story of his life, but he was also careful with the details that he gave. For example, he never mentioned his former name, his master's name, or the state and county from which he had escaped. During this time, Frederick also began to meet many influential people in the abolition movement. Among them were Samuel J. May, Wendell Phillips, and Charles Lenox Remond (after whom Frederick's fourth child was named). One person he did not get to spend much time with, however, was his wife, Anna. Some of the people in Frederick's new circle of friends tried to get Anna more involved in her husband's work. But in general, she was more comfortable being out of the public spotlight and quietly raising their children at home.

The famous abolitionist William Lloyd Garrison (1805-1879) became Frederick's mentor. Frederick embraced Garrison's philosophy of life, including his views on slavery, women's rights, and the practice of nonviolence.

Before long, Frederick started to grow bored on his long speaking tours, repeating the same story speech after speech. One time he was even scheduled to speak four times in the same day! After months of describing his experiences as a slave, Frederick decided that he wanted to do more. He was no longer satisfied with simply "narrating wrongs," as he put it. He felt he had to do something to battle the injustices of slavery. In 1842, Frederick found his chance. He learned of a man named George Latimer, who had been arrested in Boston and accused of being a fugitive slave. Frederick and Charles Remond attended a series of meetings to protest the fact that Latimer had been denied a trial by jury. Frederick was outraged by this. Though Massachusetts was a free state, its officials were in fact helping to capture runaway slaves and return them to their owners in the South. With the help of William Lloyd Garrison, Frederick raised enough money to buy Latimer's freedom. An important result of the protests in which Frederick took part was a change in Massachusetts state law. From now on, judges and law enforcement officers were no longer allowed to participate in the return of fugitive slaves.

The following year, the "Hundred Conventions" took place. This was a series of 100 antislavery meetings planned by the American Anti-Slavery Society. Although the number of meetings fell just short of the society's goal, the meetings took place throughout the North. The main purpose of the convention was to reach out to as many communities as possible and enlist new members in the antislavery movement. Along with Charles Remond and several other speakers, Frederick went on a six-month tour through the New England states, and New York, Pennsylvania, Ohio, and Indiana.

Sometimes Frederick spoke with Remond or another speaker, but just as often he traveled and spoke alone. While preaching against slavery in the South, Frederick also talked about his experiences in the North, where African Americans were segregated and treated as second-class citizens under the law. More and more, he told his audiences that bringing an end to slavery would be just the beginning of full citizenship for African Americans. Frederick's steadfast devotion to this cause brought about many controversies and conflicts with fellow abolitionists during his long life.

During his travels in upstate New York, Frederick and Charles Remond attended the National Convention of Colored Citizens. This was the first major gathering of African American men that Frederick had attended. Henry Highland Garnet gave the main speech at this meeting. Like Frederick, Henry Garnet was a former slave from the eastern shore of Maryland who escaped to the North. Ordained as a minister, he advocated a militant approach toward ending slavery. He thought slaves and free African Americans should use violent means, if necessary, to gain their freedom. Frederick and Charles Remond, however, believed in William Lloyd Garrison's philosophy of nonviolence. When Frederick stepped on the speakers' platform that day, he placed himself in opposition to Garnet's radical views. Later in life, however, Frederick became one of Garnet's vocal supporters.

. . . he told his audiences that bringing an end to slavery would be just the beginning of full citizenship for African Americans.

In September 1843, while Charles Remond stayed in Ohio, Frederick traveled to Pendleton, Indiana, with two men—George Bradburn and William A. White. Bradburn was a Unitarian minister from Massachusetts who supported abolition and women's rights, while White was a graduate of Harvard University around Frederick's age. The three of them— one black and two white—stayed in the house of a local doctor. They received threats from people who

Frederick and two fellow abolitionists were attacked by a violent mob as they were speaking in Pendleton, Indiana. Frederick's hand was broken, and it bothered him for the rest of his life.

lived in the vicinity not to give a speech in their town, but Frederick and the others paid no attention. As they were speaking, a mob of 30 or more men approached and began to throw rocks and eggs. It soon became a dangerous situation. When White was grabbed by two of the locals, Frederick found a piece of lumber to use as a club and came to his friend's rescue. A terrible fight erupted. In the end, Frederick, Bradburn, and White had to run for their lives. They were saved from further harm when a local family gave them shelter. During the attack, Frederick's right hand was broken. Unfortunately, it was not set properly and bothered him for the rest of his life.

Despite the hardships that Frederick and his fellow abolitionists experienced during their tour, the "Hundred Conventions" was a defining moment in the abolition movement. Its message of the need to end slavery in America reached a countless number of people and persuaded them to join the cause. It was also a time when Frederick came into his own as a powerful orator. Having read almost constantly during his travels, Frederick had gained an incredible education—one that had been denied him as a slave. His knowledge of the facts, his ability to persuade people, and his reputation as an orator were gradually making Frederick one of the most famous people of his day. In fact, as Frederick's fame grew, some people began to doubt if so impressive a young man could ever have been a slave. Frederick knew he had to put these doubts to rest and, in doing so, wanted to reach as wide an audience as possible. Instead of going from town to town, telling people about his life as a slave again and again, he decided to put his story in print.

My Bondage and My Freedom

In 1844, Frederick took a break from the lecture tour to write his autobiography. In fact, it would be the first of three works that told the story of his life. Taking on this monumental task also came with a good deal of risk because Frederick thought it was time to tell his full story. No longer would he conceal the facts that, up to this point, he had been careful not to reveal. He would reveal his name, the identities of the people who had owned him as a slave, and the names of the places where he had worked in bondage. Though Frederick had many powerful friends to protect him, the possibility of him being captured and returned to his owner, Thomas Auld, was a very real one. In his autobiography, Frederick wrote that he was "constantly in danger."

Frederick's first book was called *Narrative of the Life of Frederick Douglass: An American Slave* and published in 1845 by Boston's Anti-Slavery Office. It was one of the most influential pieces of literature to come out of the abolition movement. William Lloyd Garrison wrote the preface. Short and direct, the book

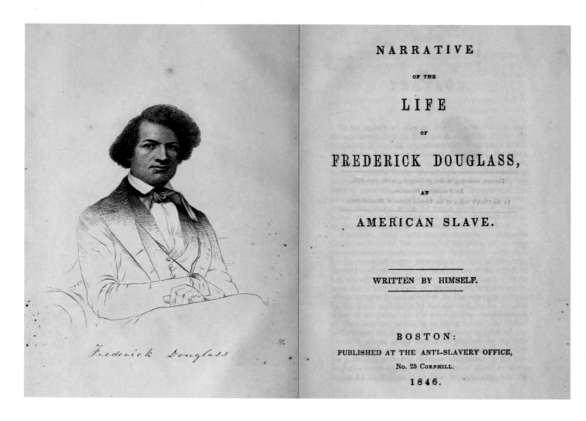

NARRATIVE

OF THE

LIFE

OF

FREDERICK DOUGLASS,

AN

AMERICAN SLAVE.

WRITTEN BY HIMSELF.

BOSTON:
PUBLISHED AT THE ANTI-SLAVERY OFFICE,
No. 25 CORNHILL.
1846.

Frederick Douglass

In 1845, Frederick published his first book, *Narrative of the Life of Frederick Douglass: An American Slave.* It was one of the most influential works of the abolition movement.

narrates Frederick's life from the time of his birth and ends with the speech he gave in Nantucket. One important detail that Frederick left out of the book was the exact means by which he escaped. He knew that if he revealed that he had eluded the authorities disguised as a sailor, it would be impossible for others who remained enslaved to use this method. He shared this detail only after the Civil War was over and slavery was officially abolished in the United States.

Ten years after writing his first autobiography, Frederick published a second one called *My Bondage and My Freedom.* Bringing up to date the account of his life after he reached the North, Frederick's second book accomplishes much more than that. It highlights the stark differences between freedom and slavery and focuses on the power of faith and literacy in people's lives. It also provides an intimate view of the inhuman system of slavery, describing what Frederick and his family had to endure at the hands of their masters. For example, when Frederick was a boy he witnessed his Aunt Hester being whipped by Captain Anthony. In the first book, the terrible event was described in a single paragraph. In the second one, however, he dedicated three full pages to it.

More than a quarter of a century later, Frederick wrote his third autobiography. Given the title *Life and Times of Frederick Douglass,* this book was not as well received by the public as his previous two. In this third book, Frederick brought the story of his life up to date and added a few interesting things he had not discussed in the previous two books. For example, he describes what it was like to be a day laborer and a skilled caulker, as well as his encounters with two presidents of the United States, Abraham Lincoln and James Garfield. Frederick also wrote extensively about the Civil War, both its causes and its far-reaching consequences for African Americans and the entire country.

The real message of Frederick's third and final book—though many people at the time were not willing to receive it—was that the story of slavery should not be erased from the nation's memory. This was something that Frederick talked about for the rest of his life. After the devastating Civil War, much of the white population of America was tired of the topic of slavery and thought that the emancipation of the slaves had taken care of the problem. Reacting to this weariness, many formerly enslaved people became almost apologetic about their past. Frederick, however, saw his life as being symbolic of a much-needed "second emancipation." But his final autobiography did not offer a plan that would meet the desperate needs of African Americans in the late 1800's.

After writing his first autobiography, Frederick fervently hoped that the book would help to shed some light on the cruelty and injustice of the American slave system. He also hoped it would hasten "the glad day of deliverance" to the millions of his brothers and sisters who were still in bondage. Frederick's friends congratulated him on his accomplishment and shared

> . . . the story of slavery should not be erased from the nation's memory. This was something that Frederick talked about for the rest of his life.

his hopes for the future. But they were nevertheless concerned that the book would put him in greater danger due to his legal status as a fugitive. His associates, especially William Lloyd Garrison, had no faith in the power of the state of Massachusetts to protect Frederick from slave hunters. Even Anna, who had helped her husband escape, could now face persecution from the law.

Frederick's associates in the abolition movement also thought that his words deserved an even wider audience—an international audience. After all, the antislavery movement was not confined to the United States. Under the black revolutionary leader Toussaint Louverture, the enslaved Africans in Haiti had freed themselves. The British government also had ended slavery in its colonies in the West Indies. In fact, West Indies Emancipation Day was celebrated on August 1 by many abolitionists in the United States. There were also close ties between abolitionists on both sides of the Atlantic. Considering the danger Frederick faced at home, his friends convinced him that it was time to go abroad.

Travels in the British Isles

Once Frederick decided to leave the United States, the question remained where he should go. To Frederick, Great Britain seemed the obvious choice. Before leaving, however, he needed to see to the welfare of his wife and four children. The Douglass family managed to make ends meet with Anna's job of repairing shoes and help from some of their friends. Frederick promised to send back as much money as he could. Some of Anna's friends also made sure that she was kept occupied while Frederick was away, inviting her to weekly meetings of a ladies' sewing group. With a heavy heart but looking toward the future, Frederick said his goodbyes to his family and booked passage on a steamer ship called the *Cambria*. The voyage would take him across the Atlantic and usher in a new chapter of his life.

Traveling across the ocean for the first time, Frederick found himself filled with high expectations. He imagined a world without barriers. At the same time, he was just anxious enough to remain cautious. Upon his arrival in Liverpool, England, Frederick was surprised by the warm reception that the city gave him. His reputation as a famous orator had preceded him, and there were many abolitionists in England who came to see him. The following day, he crossed over to Dublin, Ireland. The country was just beginning to experience what would come to be called the Great Irish Famine. As Frederick traveled through Ireland, he made many speeches against the evils of slavery and greatly impressed his audiences. In the fall of 1845, he went to Cork, a city in southern Ireland. He stayed with the Jennings family, which consisted of Thomas and Ann Jennings and their eight children. While in Cork, Frederick experienced a type of equality that he had not experienced up to that point. For the rest of his life, he remembered fondly the time he spent there.

Living in a society that was foreign to him, Frederick became aware of the stark contrast between his experiences in the United States and those in Britain. He compared the bitterness of his life as a slave and a fugitive from the law to the "wonder and amazement" of his new surroundings. Frederick also made new friends quickly. Among them was Daniel O'Connell, an Irish politician called "The Liberator" by his countrymen. O'Connell helped lead the fight for Roman Catholics to gain political rights in the mostly Protestant United Kingdom. This resulted in the passing of the Catholic Emancipation Act of 1829. Another new friend of Frederick's was Thomas Clarkson, an English abolitionist who helped end the slave trade in the British Empire. Some of Frederick's old friends— such as William Lloyd Garrison—came to see him as well. Frederick traveled extensively and gave speeches in many cities and towns throughout Ireland, England, Scotland, and Wales. He spent nearly two years in the British Isles, and they were comparatively happy ones for him.

During his time abroad, an unexpected and wonderful thing happened to Frederick—he gained his freedom from slavery once and for all. Ellen Richardson, an English abolitionist from Newcastle upon Tyne—with the help of her sister-in-law, Anna Richardson—had written to the Auld family in Maryland and began discussions about giving Frederick his freedom. Exactly how the negotiations took place is unknown, but Thomas Auld agreed to do so—for the right price, of course. Eventually, both parties settled on the sum of 150 pounds sterling (equal to $100 at the time). By December 1846, the Richardsons had managed to raise the money and the transaction was completed. Frederick was now a free man— no longer a slave or a fugitive, no longer someone else's "property" in the eyes of the law.

Frederick spent Christmas of 1846 with the Richardsons in Newcastle upon Tyne. Over the holiday, he met a young British woman named Julia Griffiths, who had dedicated herself to the cause of ending slavery. Frederick shared with her his plan to start an antislavery newspaper as soon as he returned home.

Frederick spoke out against slavery to audiences throughout Ireland, England, Scotland, and Wales. This image shows him addressing an audience in London in 1846 after he became a free man.

Julia was excited at the prospect and would eventually join Frederick in the United States to help him realize his vision. The two of them developed a close friendship that would last the rest of their lives.

Frederick had come into his own, during his travels in Great Britain. Not yet 30 years old, he had gained enormous self-confidence. For the first time in his life, he had been treated with respect in public and had experienced a life of true equality. The time spent abroad had brought him a long way toward becoming the man he had always wanted to be. At one point, Frederick considered living permanently in Edinburgh, Scotland. His friends there offered to help him settle in. Frederick, however, missed his family. He also wanted to "labor and suffer with the oppressed" of his native land. He was now ready to return to America and fight in the hard battles that lay ahead.

Return to America and *The North Star*

When the *Cambria* docked in Boston Harbor in the spring of 1847, Frederick jumped onto the dock and ran to catch the train to Lynn, Massachusetts. Less than 30 minutes later, he arrived at his home and was reunited with his family. He was met by his two sons, Lewis and Frederick Junior, who were "running and dancing with joy" to meet their father. Frederick's homecoming was a happy one.

Frederick turned his attention to the newspaper he wanted to publish. He knew it would be a challenging endeavor. However, he did not expect the challenge of publishing a newspaper to start with those he depended on. William Lloyd Garrison and some of his other friends were against the idea. They told him that starting an abolitionist newspaper would be a waste of time. One reason for this was Frederick's lack of a formal education. This upset Frederick very much, but he persisted. He felt that he could make up for it through further study and that "wisdom would come by experience." He was convinced that a newspaper published by African Americans was a necessary step on the road to ending slavery. Frederick came to think that Massachusetts might not be the best place to publish his newspaper. Feeling that he needed a fresh start, he decided to move his family to Rochester, New York.

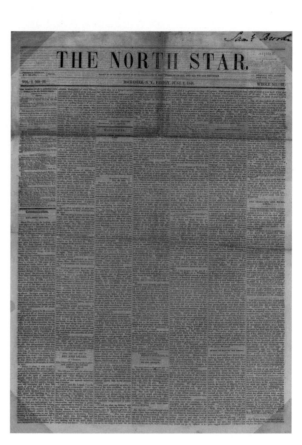

Frederick published his first newspaper, *The North Star*, on Dec. 3, 1847. The paper's name was a reference to the star that many runaway slaves followed at night as they made their way to freedom.

In 1847, Rochester was a prosperous city of 50,000 people, located in upstate New York near Lake Ontario. Just across the lake was Canada—the last, safe stop of the underground railroad. The move was a difficult one for the Douglass family. For one reason, they were leaving behind their circle of friends. Another was that prejudice against free African Americans was very strong in Rochester. Despite the trials they faced, Frederick, Anna, and their children settled into their new home. Uprooted once again by her husband, Anna found herself in a strange city. One of her greatest comforts during these years was the garden she established wherever home was, gardens she tended with loving care.

Rochester's A.M.E. Zion Church was a couple of miles from the Douglass home. Frederick set up his newspaper office in the church's basement. He chose the name *The North Star* for his publication. This was a reference to the star that many runaway slaves followed at night as they made their way to freedom. The newspaper was first published on December 3, 1847. It had subscribers throughout the United States, Great Britain, and the West Indies. While finances remained a concern, Frederick's dedicated colleagues, such as Julia Griffiths, worked endlessly to raise funds to support the newspaper. *The North Star* would remain in circulation until 1851, when it merged with Gerrit Smith's *Liberty Party Paper* to form *Frederick Douglass' Paper*.

Frederick's newspaper venture had one unfortunate outcome, however. His long association with friend and mentor, William Lloyd Garrison, ended in disagreement. Garrison had come to believe that the U.S. Constitution was a pro-slavery document and urged his supporters not to take part in elections.

After reading the Constitution himself, Frederick came to the opposite conclusion. He saw no proof that the Constitution supported slavery. He believed it was therefore the duty and privilege of every citizen to vote—if the government had given them the right to do so. Along with growing political differences, there was another reason for the split between the two men—Frederick's newspaper competed with Garrison's own paper. Despite his falling-out with Garrison, Frederick's *The North Star* proved to be a success and further established his name in the movement to end slavery.

CHAPTER 3

The Coming Civil War

The Changing Political Climate

Frederick was never away from the lecture circuit for very long, despite the burdens of being a newspaper publisher, a husband, and a father of four children (with a fifth one on the way). Wherever he went, Frederick spoke against slavery and urged his listeners to subscribe to *The North Star*. Around this time, another political movement began to gain in strength. Its goal was to achieve equal rights for men and women. The movement was led by such remarkable and influential women as Elizabeth Cady Stanton, Lucretia Mott, and Susan B. Anthony. In July 1848, Frederick went to the Seneca Falls Convention, the first women's rights convention in the United States, held in Seneca Falls, New York. He was the only African American abolitionist to attend. This convention was planned by Elizabeth Cady Stanton. She, along with her Declaration of Sentiments, helped to gain equality for women at a time when a woman's traditional role in society—caring for the home and children—was very much entrenched. Frederick knew it was only fair for women to have a voice in American politics and lent his considerable support to Stanton. He knew it was not right to fight for full citizenship as an African American man if women were to be denied the same right. After the convention, he used *The North Star* to make the case for women's rights.

The country was beginning to change. During this time, some of Frederick's ideas changed as well, especially after he formally broke ties with William Lloyd Garrison in 1851. One example was his view on the underground railroad. Though Frederick himself had made use of the organization during his escape to the

He knew it was not right to fight for full citizenship as an African American man if women were to be denied the same right.

North, he more and more began to call it the "upper-ground railroad." Though he continued to believe in the importance of the underground railroad, he never approved of the public way in which some of his friends openly talked about it, pointing out that its "stations" were far better known by the slaveholders than the enslaved. He called upon his fellow abolitionists to do nothing to hinder his enslaved brothers and sisters in making their attempt to escape bondage.

1n 1850, a crisis gripped the country and moved it toward what would be the Civil War. The United States was a growing nation. After the Mexican–American War (1846–1848), it had gained a lot of new territory—about half of Mexico, in fact. With this newly acquired land came an intense political struggle

This image of Frederick Douglass was taken around 1850, as a crisis over slavery gripped the country. The Compromise of 1850 attempted to resolve the issue.

between the slave states in the South and the free states in the North. Politicians in the South wanted the new states that were to be carved out of Mexico's former territory to be slave states. But abolitionists wanted the new states to outlaw slavery. The Compromise of 1850, negotiated by senators Henry Clay and Stephen Douglas, attempted to resolve the issue. However, part of this compromise was the controversial Fugitive Slave Act.

The Fugitive Slave Act proposed that fugitive slaves had no right to a trial by jury and could not testify in their own defense. Essentially, one white person's word was enough to accuse someone of being a fugitive—even if he or she was a free black—and send him or her into slavery. Once this act was passed by the Congress and became law, it deeply affected Frederick and all other free African Americans. Men, women, and children living in the North were now in danger more than ever before. Fear became so pervasive among free blacks that many of them simply lost hope. It was difficult for some people to believe that their nation's government could be so shortsighted. While many in the African American community decided to move to Canada, Frederick was determined to stay and fight. He traveled far and wide giving fiery speeches denouncing the new law. Despite his earlier criticism regarding the underground railroad, he and

Anna now made their Rochester home one of its official stops.

In 1852, Frederick was invited to address the Rochester Ladies' Anti-Slavery Society on Independence Day. He agreed to speak, but not on that date. He insisted on speaking one day later, and a great crowd flocked to see him in Corinthian Hall. In the fiery lecture he gave that day, Frederick told his audience that the Fourth of July "is yours, not mine." He added that though many rejoiced on July 4, he would mourn. He pointed out how the many positive values of the American system, such as freedom and citizenship, were simply not seen in the same light by enslaved and free African Americans. The obvious and understandable reason for this was that they were prohibited from fully exercising these rights. Therefore, how could he join in the holiday that celebrated the nation's birth when millions of Americans were denied freedom? This address, which became known as his "Fifth of July Speech," was one of the most powerful Frederick would ever give against slavery and injustice.

While many in the African American community decided to move to Canada, Frederick was determined to stay and fight.

Frederick also came to believe that education was the key to improving the lives of former slaves and other African Americans—in fact, all people. By the 1850's, he saw that schools for African American children in the state of New York were vastly inferior to the ones for white children. He was an early advocate for the desegregation of schools and called for action in the courts to achieve this goal.

Dred Scott and John Brown

Frederick became more and more active in politics. He joined the Liberty Party, which had broken away from the American Anti-Slavery Society. He spoke at the party's conventions and took on a leadership role. Around this time, he also published his second autobiography, *My Bondage and My Freedom*.

In 1857, Frederick was alarmed by the controversial decision of the U.S. Supreme Court in the case of Dred Scott. Scott was a slave who was taken by his owner to live in a state where slavery was illegal. By keeping Scott as a slave in a free state, his owner was breaking the law. Later, Scott's owner moved back to a state where slavery was practiced, taking Scott with him. When his master died, Scott was considered the property of his master's widow. However, Scott argued that, because he once lived in a free state, he should be set free, along with his wife and two daughters. Scott decided to sue his former master's widow to gain his freedom. Unfortunately, the courts declared that, as a slave, he wasn't considered an American citizen. He was therefore not protected by the law and thus could not sue anyone. When the Supreme Court handed down its decision, Frederick gave a speech in which he condemned the government's action. He declared that all African Americans, both slave and free, were citizens of the United States.

In October 1859, another shocking event rocked the country. At the time, Frederick was in Philadelphia. He was about to give a speech at National Hall when he received news about an attack on a U.S. arsenal in Harpers Ferry, Virginia. Most surprising of all was that the man behind the raid was John Brown, a fellow abolitionist and one of Frederick's friends! Attempting to steal weapons from the arsenal, Brown planned to launch an armed slave revolt.

Frederick first met John Brown in 1848. Brown, who was then living in Springfield, Massachusetts, had invited Frederick to visit his home. Because Brown was famous in the abolition movement, Frederick was pleased at the invitation and eager to meet him. During their visit, Brown denounced slavery as a great evil. He told Frederick that slavery would never be ended by giving speeches or through political

The radical abolitionist John Brown (1800-1859) and his followers were captured after a raid on the U.S. arsenal at Harpers Ferry, Virginia. Brown was later hanged for treason.

means. It would take an armed rebellion. Brown shared his plans with Frederick. Brown intended to raid plantations and set free as many slaves as possible. He even invited Frederick to take part in his plot. Frederick refused but wondered if Brown had the right idea. Later, Brown gained nationwide fame in a border war between the opponents and supporters of slavery known as "Bleeding Kansas."

When Frederick heard about the raid on Harpers Ferry, he knew that Brown had finally acted on his idea of ending slavery through violent means. The next day Frederick learned that a Virginia regiment under Colonel Robert E. Lee, who later became the leading general of the secessionist Confederate States, had captured Brown. Upon his arrest, Brown was searched and some of Frederick's letters were found on him. When Frederick's friends and neighbors heard the news, they urged him to flee the country. Although Frederick had taken no part in Brown's raid, he knew he would likely be arrested because of his association with Brown. He also knew he would never receive a fair trial. The following day, U.S. marshals arrived at Frederick's home in Rochester. Frederick, however, was already gone. Stopping only briefly in Canada, Frederick returned to Great Britain and lived there for several months. Once again, he gave many antislavery speeches and spoke about John Brown's raid. In December 1859, Frederick learned that Brown had been executed by the U.S. government

> *He believed that Brown's zeal for African Americans was greater than his own.*

for treason. Frederick wrote eloquently about his friend following the Civil War. He believed that Brown's zeal for African Americans was greater than his own. "I could live for the slave," he said, "but [Brown] could die for him." While in Britain, Frederick received even worse news—his beloved daughter Annie had died after a brief illness, just nine days before her 11th birthday. Anna, alone with the other four children, was inconsolable. Frederick's grief was profound. He had to return home, despite knowing that he could be arrested if he set foot in the United States. Frederick boarded the first outgoing ship to Portland, Maine. Once back in Rochester with his family, he lived in secret for nearly a month. By this time, however, the government seemed to have lost interest in Frederick's case. There were greater problems on the horizon.

Abraham Lincoln and the Outbreak of War

The great division between the slave states in the South and the free states in the North had been growing for a long time—as well as their separate visions for the future of the country. Frederick could see that the ideas he was helping to spread were beginning to move the nation. The debate centered on whether slavery should be expanded, and it was slowly splitting the United States in two. Inevitably, the slavery issue moved toward conflict. The presidential election of 1860 became the turning point. That year, the Republican Party, which had been founded only six years earlier, nominated Abraham Lincoln, an Illinois lawyer, to be president.

Frederick could not know it at the time, but he and Lincoln would become partners in the struggle to end slavery. Frederick also learned he had a few things in common with Lincoln. Both had taught themselves to read and became dazzling orators, yet there were obvious differences. Lincoln was a politician, while Frederick was a reformer. Lincoln spent most of his life trying to rid the nation of slavery, but he remained doubtful African Americans could become full and equal citizens. This was something Frederick fought for until his dying day. At the same time, Frederick recognized that the Republican Party was far from being an abolitionist movement. However, he saw that the party of Lincoln carried "the antislavery sentiment of the North."

Frederick could not know it at the time, but he and Lincoln would become partners in the struggle to end slavery.

He knew a Republican victory at the polls would mean a victory against slavery. Many people in the South shared this view of Lincoln as well. They understood that he represented a threat to the South's economy (which was based on slavery) and whole way of life.

On November 6, 1860, Abraham Lincoln was elected to become the 16th president of the United States. The following month, South Carolina seceded (withdrew) from the Union in open defiance. Six more states followed suit before Lincoln took office on March 4, 1861. (In total, 11 states would break away to form the Confederate States of America.) On April 12, Confederate forces in South Carolina attacked Union soldiers stationed at Fort Sumter, a United States military base in Charleston Harbor. The Civil War had begun. When Frederick heard the news, he momentarily rejoiced. He knew the time had come to break the chains of slavery once and for all.

In time, Frederick saw the horrors that war always produces and called for it to be ended as quickly as possible. One of the best ways to do this would be to enlist African American soldiers to the Union cause. After all, the Confederacy was using enslaved people

On April 12, 1861, Confederate forces fired on Fort Sumter, the U.S. military base in Charleston, South Carolina. Frederick momentarily rejoiced when he heard the Civil War had begun.

Frederick was one of the many signers of such posters as this one recruiting African American men to fight in the Union Army.

to support its army. Frederick spoke about this idea throughout the Northern States. However, Frederick faced a good deal of resistance. He knew that prejudice against African Americans was alive and well in the North. It was not going to be easy to convince the political leaders of his day to integrate black soldiers into the Union army.

As it turned out, it took years of devastating war for America's political leaders to realize what Frederick had known from the beginning. The Union took a small step toward integrating black soldiers into its ranks when Lincoln approved the enlistment of 50,000 African Americans to build fortifications, perform scouting missions, and so on. In May 1863, the War Department authorized the United States Colored Troops (USCT), a corps of black soldiers under the leadership of white officers. Frederick traveled throughout the North to help in the recruitment process. Two of his sons, Lewis and Charles, were among the first to sign up from the state of New York, and Frederick Junior served as a

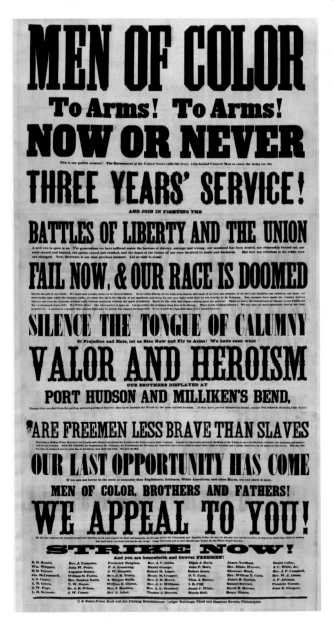

recruiter. One of the USCT's greatest moments in the war, in which Lewis took part, was the Second Battle of Fort Wagner. Though a tactical defeat, the battle proved beyond any doubt the fighting capabilities of African American soldiers. By 1865, nearly 178,000 black soldiers had taken part in the war, making up almost one-tenth of the Union army.

Emancipation and the End of the War

Frederick's other main idea to end the war quickly was to emancipate, or set free, every slave in the United States. He wrote numerous articles in his newspaper, pressuring President Lincoln and leaders in Congress to free the slaves and enlist African American soldiers. Eventually, Frederick made progress on this point as well. Lincoln, along with some of his generals and fellow politicians in Washington, began to understand that freeing the slaves was the right thing to do. It would also deliver a heavy blow to the leaders of the Confederacy when they realized African Americans were helping to fight the war.

In the fall of 1862, President Lincoln finally announced his intentions to free the slaves! Lincoln's Emancipation Proclamation would go into effect on New Year's Day 1863. It declared that all slaves in Confederate-held territory were to be set free. (Slaves in the North were not freed until the adoption of the Thirteenth Amendment to the Constitution in December 1865.) Frederick and his fellow abolitionists were jubilant at the news. It was news they had waited their whole lives to hear. On January 1, Frederick found himself in Boston. A great crowd gathered at

Tremont Temple to celebrate President Lincoln's monumental announcement. Suddenly, a man made his way through the assembly and exclaimed, "It is on the wires!" The announcement was being circulated by telegraph. The people who were gathered there cheered. Frederick was ecstatic, calling the Emancipation Proclamation "the turning-point between freedom and slavery." It was celebrated throughout the Northern States.

On August 10, 1863, Frederick traveled to Washington, D.C., to meet with Lincoln. He was uncertain about the prospects of the meeting, but he felt compelled to "lay the complaints of my people before President Lincoln." The meeting was a great moment in the history of the United States. Lincoln invited Frederick into the White House at a time when most white people wouldn't let an African American cross the threshold of their homes. Frederick received a warm welcome from President Lincoln and was deeply impressed by him. Immediately Frederick felt that the word "honest" was correctly applied to Lincoln. Frederick began the conversation by thanking the president for everything he had done for slaves and African American soldiers. When he claimed that the government was not treating the soldiers fairly, however, Lincoln asked him to explain. Frederick went on to say that the men of the USCT didn't receive the same pay or protection upon capture as their white counterparts did. He also wanted them to receive the same rewards for heroic action on the battlefield. Lincoln listened intently to what his guest had to say, and Frederick came away from the meeting feel-

ing elated. By the end of the war, African American soldiers had received everything Frederick asked for.

During another visit to the White House, Frederick spoke with President Lincoln at greater length. Lincoln expressed his disappointment that more African Americans had not joined up with the Union forces. He and Frederick discussed plans about how to change that. The two men shared their concerns about how the Civil War might end and what would happen once it was over. More than most, Frederick understood that winning the war would not bring an end to prejudice. During their conversation, Frederick was impressed with the president's deep, moral convictions against slavery. Of course, the two of them did not agree on everything. For example, Lincoln never publicly endorsed suffrage, or the right to vote, for freed black men and was in favor of them return-

On Jan. 1, 1863, President Lincoln (third from left) issued the Emancipation Proclamation that led to the end of slavery in the United States. Frederick was ecstatic over the news.

ing to Africa. Frederick was vehemently against both of these notions. Nevertheless, both men maintained a high degree of respect for the other.

In April 1865, the Civil War came to an end when the Confederate General Robert E. Lee surrendered to Union forces under General Ulysses S. Grant at the home of Wilmer McLean in Appomattox Court House, Virginia. It had been a terrible struggle in which hundreds of thousands of people had died. Frederick rejoiced with the rest of the nation that it was finally over. But then tragedy struck. Frederick was in Rochester when news came that President Lincoln had been assassinated. While attending a play at Ford's Theatre in Washington, the president was shot by John Wilkes Booth. Booth was a famous actor who supported the Confederacy. He strongly opposed the abolition of slavery in America. Frederick was stunned and overwhelmed by the terrible news. He called Lincoln's assassination "a crime and calamity hitherto unknown to our country." His joy at the end of the war was now "tinged with a feeling of sadness."

If not for an assassin's bullet, Frederick would likely have continued his partnership with Lincoln. Yet, despite the president's death, slavery had come to an end. No African American man, woman, or child would ever be sold into bondage again. Family members would no longer be split up due to the inhuman institution that had lasted for more than 400 years in the American colonies and then in the United States. African Americans had yet to gain full and equal citizenship, but many people, including Frederick, remained hopeful about the future.

CHAPTER 4

The Struggle for Emancipation

The Era of Reconstruction and "Jim Crow"

After the Civil War, freed blacks, such as these, faced many obstacles. Throughout the South, laws were passed to enforce racial segregation. These laws were known as "Jim Crow" laws.

In 1865, the Civil War came to an end and emancipation had been won. Many people throughout the United States thought their country would become a land of equality and opportunity for all its citizens. William Lloyd Garrison, one of the people who had helped bring slavery to an end, thought the struggle was over. For him, with the liberation of the slaves, he felt his job was done and called for the American Anti-Slavery Society to be disbanded. Frederick, however, recognized that the era of freedom he fought so hard to establish had not yet arrived. Slavery was no longer a legal institution, but there was still a lot of work to be done to overturn racial injustice.

Though the war was over, the country remained divided. Eleven states had seceded to form the Confederacy. With its defeat, these states were left occupied by Union forces, and the country entered the period known as Reconstruction. The nation had to be rebuilt, and there were competing ideas about how to do this. One view, held by the so-called "Radical Republicans," called for full citizenship for African Americans. Another view, which was held by many people in the North and the South, did not believe that African Americans deserved equal rights. A third view recognized that the war had been a traumatic experience (even for the former Confederate States) and called for national reconciliation. Like Abraham Lincoln, the new president, Andrew Johnson, was in favor of bringing the Southern States back into the Union as quickly as possible.

Frederick and Anna were eager to start a new life. Frederick was now in his late 40's, Anna her early 50's, and their children were in their 20's. By now, Frederick was a famous man—a man whose advice President Lincoln had once sought. The war-torn people of the United States, still dealing with grief and loss, looked to Frederick for leadership and inspiration. Invitations to speak continued to pour in. Around this time, Frederick developed ties with the newly founded Freedman's Savings and Trust Company. Also known as the Freedman's Savings Bank, it assisted in the economic development of newly emancipated African Americans after the Civil War. Frederick briefly served as the bank's president, but unfortunately it went bankrupt just a few months after he took office.

This was a difficult time for Frederick and the country in general. He faced prejudice nearly everywhere he went. There was tremendous political unrest. New white supremacist groups, such as the Ku Klux Klan, appeared in the South and waged a war of terror and violence against the freed slaves. As time went by, it became obvious that the struggle of African Americans was far from over. The institution of slavery had been outlawed, but former slaveholders were doing everything they could to limit the newly gained rights of their former slaves.

Throughout the South, state and local laws were passed that enforced racial segregation. These new laws required blacks to be separated from whites in all public places. The principle of "separate but equal" became the rule of the day. New laws on labor and the punishment of criminal acts also served to disenfranchise the black population of the South. This series of regulations, which effectively made African Americans second-class citizens, came to be known as "Jim Crow" laws. ("Jim Crow" was a derogatory term used for African Americans at the time.) Frederick had long feared that the recent progress he and others had helped to achieve would be rolled back in this way. He even predicted it during the Civil War.

The Power of the Vote

To counter these new tactics to restrict the rights of African Americans, Frederick knew what had to be done. The right to vote would have to be won. To champion this important cause, he traveled throughout the country and delivered powerful speeches calling for African American men to be given the right to vote. Accompanied by a delegation that included his son Lewis, Frederick went to Washington and met with President Andrew Johnson to discuss the matter. Afterward, Frederick's delegation wrote a letter to the U.S. Senate, urging its members to support their cause.

In the summer of 1866, the National Union Convention took place in Philadelphia. It was called primarily to gain support for the policies of President Johnson. The president's mild policies toward the South faced stiff opposition from the Radical Republicans, who

As time went by, it became obvious that the struggle of African Americans was far from over.

wanted to punish the South and win voting rights for former slaves. To his great surprise, Frederick was chosen by his adopted hometown of Rochester to be a delegate at the convention. He spoke eloquently in favor of giving African American men the right to vote. However, many others disagreed with his views. The convention proved unsuccessful in rallying support behind President Johnson. Frederick's passion for African American suffrage did not diminish. In fact, it became all-consuming.

Before he left Philadelphia, Frederick had an amazing encounter. One day, as he was walking down Chestnut Street on the way to the convention, he spotted someone he knew in the crowd. It was Amanda Auld Sears, the daughter of his former owners, Thomas and Lucretia Auld. Greatly surprised, Frederick rushed toward her and asked her what she was doing in Philadelphia. "I heard you were to be here," Amanda replied. It was a happy reunion, and it made Frederick realize the world had changed, indeed.

The Fourteenth Amendment to the Constitution took effect on July 9, 1868. It granted citizenship rights and equal protection under the law to African Americans. Around this time, Frederick had a falling-out with another old friend, Elizabeth Cady Stanton of the women's rights movement. Stanton was discouraged by Frederick's fight to gain suffrage for African American men. She supported universal suffrage. She thought everyone—men and women, black and white—should have the right to vote. Frederick believed in this as well, but in his mind the Civil War would have been fought in vain if African Americans continued to be denied the right to vote. He thought this fight should therefore take precedence. Finally, in 1870, the Fifteenth Amendment to the Constitution was ratified, giving African American men the right to vote. It was another important step forward in the history of the United States. Frederick had fought long and hard to win this victory.

American Statesman

By this time, Frederick had become a giant in the American political arena. He had won many victories in the battle for freedom and civil rights. Two presidents of the United States had sought his counsel. In 1868, Frederick used his considerable influence and backed Ulysses S. Grant, the former Union general, in the presidential election that year. Once in office, Grant signed the Enforcement Acts, which protected

CELEBRATION AT BALTIMORE ON MAY 19th 1870.

THE FIFTEENTH AMENDMENT AND ITS RESULTS.

African Americans' rights to vote, to hold office, to serve on juries, and to receive equal protection under the law. This made President Grant highly unpopular in the eyes of many white people, but it earned him Frederick's praise.

President Grant rewarded Frederick for his support. In 1871, Grant made him Commissioner to Santo Domingo in the Dominican Republic. Over the years, Frederick served a total of four U.S. presidents in various roles. Rutherford B. Hayes appointed Frederick U.S. marshal for the District of Columbia in 1877. James Garfield appointed him recorder of deeds

The Fifteenth Amendment to the Constitution gave black men the right to vote. It was ratified in 1870. Frederick (bottom left) had fought long and hard to win this victory.

for the District of Columbia in 1881, and Benjamin Harrison appointed Frederick minister resident and consul general to the Republic of Haiti in 1889.

In 1872, the Equal Rights Party chose Victoria Woodhull as its nominee for president. The party chose Frederick to be her running mate. This made him the first African American to be nominated for vice president of the United States. Despite this honor, Frederick's nomination was made without his approval, and he never campaigned for the Equal Rights Party. Remaining loyal to President Grant, he supported his re-election bid. Frederick was also a presidential elector for the state of New York.

In 1872, Frederick became the first African American to be nominated for vice president of the United States when the Equal Rights Party presidential nominee Victoria Woodhull (1838-1927) chose him as her running mate.

Sadly, Frederick's home in Rochester burned down in June of that year. Arson was immediately suspected. Rushing to the scene, Frederick was relieved to find his family safe. Anna, with the help of their daughter Rosetta, had managed to save a few items. However, their home, most of their possessions, and Frederick's important papers all went up in flames. Among the items that were lost were the only existing and complete collections of *The North Star, Frederick Douglass' Paper,* and *Douglass' Monthly* (his third newspaper), along with hundreds of personal letters. Virtually everything that Frederick had published, from 1848 to 1860, had been reduced to ash. Frederick was heartbroken and devastated by the tremendous loss.

After the fire, he and Anna weighed their options and decided it was time for yet another move. They would leave Rochester behind and make their way to Washington, D.C. It proved to be an exciting time to live in the nation's capital. For the first time in the country's history, African Americans enjoyed positions of power and influence. By the end of the 1800's, more than 20 African American men had served in Congress. Frederick was now looked upon as one of the nation's foremost leaders.

The Unveiling of the Freedman's Memorial

On April 14, 1876, Frederick was invited to give the keynote address at the unveiling of a new monument in Washington. The Emancipation Memorial, popularly known as the Freedman's Memorial, was designed and created by the sculptor Thomas Ball. It portrays Abraham Lincoln in his role as the "Great Emancipator," holding the celebrated proclamation with which he set the slaves free. Next to Lincoln is a male African American freed slave. The former slave, wearing only a loincloth and broken shackles, is down on one knee at the president's feet. One of his hands is balled into a fist. At the base of the monument is a single word: EMANCIPATION. The monument was paid for over the course of a decade through small donations made by freed African American men and women from all over the South, including many veterans of the Civil War. The sculpture was commonly referred to as the "Lincoln Memorial" before the famous building known by that name today was completed in 1922.

When the new Freedman's Memorial was unveiled in 1876, Frederick did not like it. To him, the figure of the kneeling enslaved man represented a gesture of supplication (pleading) to whites for deliverance from bondage.

The date chosen for the unveiling of this monument was the 11th anniversary of Lincoln's assassination. A group of prominent men, including President Grant, members of Congress and the Supreme Court, and a few African American leaders, gathered for the occasion. There was also a crowd of some 25,000 people, the great majority of whom were African American. During the opening ceremonies, the band played a rousing rendition of "Hail, Columbia" (this was the unofficial national anthem until 1931, when "The Star-Spangled Banner" took its place). After a moment of silence, President Grant approached the monument, still covered by U.S. flags, and pulled the cord to unveil this new memorial. The crowd cheered and the band played "Hail to the Chief."

Stepping onto the speakers' platform, Frederick took a moment to look upon the memorial. He did not like it. A kneeling slave had been a symbol of the abolitionist movement from the beginning, but times had changed. To Frederick, and many other people, the image represented a gesture of supplication (pleading)—to whites and perhaps to God—for deliverance from bondage. As he began to speak, Frederick gently warned his listeners

A kneeling slave had been a symbol of the abolitionist movement from the beginning, but times had changed.

that it was only fair to speak the truth as he and many people in the African American community saw it. He then proclaimed Lincoln to be "the white man's president." He himself was a white man and "shared the prejudices common to his countrymen." Frederick went on to recite a well-rehearsed litany of the many criticisms that he had hurled against Lincoln during his presidency. This, of course, shocked many people in the crowd. They had expected Frederick to heap praise on Lincoln's name, not to condemn his legacy.

Then slowly Frederick began to change his tone, and when he finished his speech the crowd gave him a standing ovation. Frederick went on to point out that while white Americans had very good reasons to honor Lincoln, African Americans had reasons of their own. "Lincoln saved for you a country," Frederick told his white audience, but he delivered African

Americans from bondage. The bondage of slavery, he said, was "worse than ages of the oppression" the Founding Fathers had rebelled against. From the beginning of the Civil War, African Americans had understood this. For this reason, they never lost faith in Lincoln. Every criticism that Frederick raised against Lincoln in the first part of his speech was now placed in a greater context. Each of them was based on a "partial and imperfect" understanding of the man who had freed the slaves. The president had been a politician, not a reformer. He therefore reflected the values and beliefs of the people who had elected him to high office. Lincoln may have loved the Union more than he hated slavery, but he did hate it. In the end, Lincoln's mission had been twofold: to restore the Union and to "free his country from the great crime of slavery."

The famous speech that Frederick gave that day also echoed his own career and evolution of thought. Starting out as an unyielding abolitionist, he went on to become one of the leading voices in the African American community and was now a loyal member of the party of Lincoln. Often viewed as a harsh critique of the president, this speech captures how Frederick saw not just the "Great Emancipator," but also himself and the country in general. He understood the limits of American democracy. He praised Lincoln for the great deeds he managed to accomplish. Frederick's evaluation of Lincoln that day has rarely been matched. It serves as a reminder that the greatest statesmen of every time and place must exemplify the high ideals of the reformer, while at the same time earning the trust of the whole people.

FROM THE PLANTATION TO THE SENATE.

Later Years in Washington, D.C.

In 1877, Frederick returned to his roots. Nearly 30 years earlier, on the 10th anniversary of his escape, he had written to his former master, Thomas Auld. In his emotional letter, Frederick pleaded for information about family members who remained in bondage. He asked Auld if his grandmother was still alive and, if so, to send her to live with him in Rochester, where he would love and care for the woman who had raised him. Frederick never received a reply. After his appointment as U.S. marshal for the District of Columbia by President Hayes, Frederick decided to return home for a long overdue visit.

When he arrived in Talbot County, Frederick received an unexpected invitation. Thomas Auld, now in his 80's and very ill, had heard that Frederick was in the area and asked if he would come for a visit. Immediately Frederick accepted the invitation. He was more than willing to meet with Auld now that the two of them, former slave and former master, "stood upon equal ground." Despite Auld's harsh treatment of him years ago, Frederick held no grudges. Like himself, Frederick regarded Auld as "a victim of the circumstances of birth, education, law, and custom." Upon meeting, the two men shook hands. Auld wept, and Frederick was so moved that he could not speak at first. They talked about many things, among which was Frederick's lifelong quest for information about his birth. Frederick calculated that he had been born in 1817. Auld, whose mind was still strong, told him it had been in February 1818. (This was verified a century later when Aaron Anthony's slave records were

examined.) During the 20-minute encounter, the two men reconciled. Some members of the African American community criticized Frederick for meeting with his former slave master. Frederick, however, neither regretted nor forgot that remarkable day. Thomas Auld died shortly afterward.

Several years later, Frederick returned once more to Maryland's eastern shore to visit Colonel Edward Lloyd's plantation. He had not been there since he was about 7 years old and sent to live in Baltimore to work for Hugh Auld. Frederick was hesitant to make this visit. He was unsure how he would be received by Colonel Lloyd's descendants, but his friends encouraged him to go. Frederick's anxiety, however, soon came to an end. When he arrived at the plantation, he was greeted warmly by the Lloyd family. Among

In 1878, Frederick moved to his last home, which he named Cedar Hill, overlooking the Anacostia River in Washington, D.C. It is now a national historic site.

Frederick's hosts was young Howard Lloyd, the great-grandson of the colonel. Frederick was greatly surprised to see how little about the place had changed. The group visited the cemetery on the grounds where Colonel Lloyd was buried and then went inside Wye House, where Frederick and his friends were offered some refreshment. Before leaving, some people who lived nearby came by to see Frederick, as they had heard he was visiting. Many of them were the children of the former slaves who had once worked on the plantation. Like his visit with Thomas Auld, this was an emotional time for Frederick. It gave him a sense of peace and closure to that chapter of his life.

In 1878, Frederick and Anna moved yet again—and for the last time. The couple bought a beautiful house on a hill in the District of Columbia overlooking the Anacostia River. They named it Cedar Hill. After moving there, Frederick earned a nickname that stayed with him for the rest of his life. With a powerful physique and full head of hair (which by now had turned snowy white), he became known as the "Lion of Anacostia." By this time, Frederick and Anna were in their 60's. Their children were grown and raising families of their own. Rosetta, their oldest, had married Nathan Sprague and was living in Rochester. When

Frederick, with a powerful build and full head of hair, became known as the "Lion of Anacostia" in Washington, D.C.

her parents moved to Washington, however, she followed to be close to them. Lewis Douglass was often at his father's side at political functions in the nation's capital. He married Helen Loguen, the daughter of a renowned bishop of the A.M.E. Zion Church. Lewis also served in government before starting a career in real estate. After the Civil War, Frederick Junior married Virginia Hewlett and served as a court bailiff in Washington. Charles, like his father and older brother Lewis, was also active in government and politics. Frederick and Anna were very proud of their children and ready to enjoy their golden years.

Frederick and Anna loved their new home. Every morning he would walk five miles on the 15-acre estate and gaze at the dome of the nearby U.S. Capitol building. Frederick also surrounded himself with books at Cedar Hill to continue his lifelong pursuit of educating himself. With a collection of over 2,000 volumes, he filled his bookshelves until they overflowed. The Douglass children and grandchildren visited Cedar Hill often, sometimes for months at a time, and the house was quickly expanded from 14 to 21 rooms. Important officials from Washington, as well as family friends, stopped by Cedar Hill on a regular basis. A great storyteller, Frederick would weave wonderful tales for the people who came to see him and Anna. One of their grandsons, Joseph, was a concert violinist. He often entertained visitors with his beautiful music during their stay. There was always good conversation, lively music, and a delicious meal at Cedar Hill. During this time, Frederick began to work on his third and final autobiography. *Life and*

Times of Frederick Douglass was published in 1881.

The following year, Anna's health began to fail. It had been in decline for some time, as she suffered from severe rheumatism. In July, she had a stroke and became gravely ill. Sadly, she never recovered. On August 4, 1882, the matriarch of the Douglass family passed away. Frederick was grief-stricken and inconsolable. The woman who had helped him escape from slavery, given birth to his five children, and provided a stable home for almost 44 years—in good times and bad—was now gone. Upon her death, Frederick went into mourning and struggled with depression for more than a year.

When Frederick became the recorder of deeds for the administration of President Garfield in 1881, he had hired a 45-year-old white woman named Helen Pitts from Honeoye, New York, to serve as his clerk. Helen was a descendant of John and Priscilla Alden, who sailed to America aboard the *Mayflower*. Helen came from a prestigious family and had taken part in the struggle to end slavery. She believed in the equality of the races and was a fervent supporter of women's rights. She also helped Frederick deal with the loss of Anna. It was not long before the two of them became close. On January 24, 1884, Frederick and Helen were married. Unfortunately, their marriage was poorly received by the public as well as some family and friends. After a lifetime of battling prejudice, Frederick and his new wife took the criticism in stride. Frederick pointed out that Anna had been the color of his mother, while Helen was the color of his father. Summing up her feelings for Frederick, Helen said, "Love came to me, and I was not afraid to marry the man I loved because of his color." One major source of support for the newlywed couple was Elizabeth Cady Stanton, who had reconciled with Frederick since their split years earlier on how best to achieve universal suffrage. Stanton defended Frederick and Helen's marriage, quoting the basic principles on which the American way of life was founded. She believed everyone ought to have the right to marry whom they please, regardless of their race, creed, or class.

Frederick and Helen had a wonderful marriage. While he and Anna had little in common after leaving Baltimore, he and Helen had many things in

common. Among their shared interests were literature, music, and travel. In September 1886, the newlyweds decided to take a grand tour of Europe. Crossing the Atlantic, the couple started off in the British Isles. This was their first stop on a journey that would last nearly a year. On his third visit to Great Britain, Frederick was reunited with the old friends he had made during his years in exile. In Ireland, he spoke in defense of Irish home rule. Under home rule, Ireland

In 1884, Frederick married Helen Pitts (1838-1903), seated on the right, a white woman from a prestigious family, who had taken part in the struggle to end slavery.

would remain part of the United Kingdom, which would control Ireland's defense and foreign policy, as well as its taxes. However, Ireland would have its own parliament to deal with Irish affairs. Following a stay in London, Frederick and Helen moved on to Paris and then to Rome. They toured the Italian countryside, then decided to extend their tour and traveled across the Mediterranean Sea to Egypt. In the "land of the pharaohs," Frederick went into the desert and saw the pyramids and the Great Sphinx on the Giza plateau. He even climbed to the top of the Great Pyramid. As he looked down at the crumbling buildings of that ancient site, Frederick was reminded of just how ancient the institution of slavery was. It was a deeply moving experience for him. In August 1887, after the trip of a lifetime, he and Helen returned home to Cedar Hill.

Back in the United States, Frederick continued to travel and gave lectures everywhere he went. In 1888, he attended the Republican National Convention, which nominated Benjamin Harrison for president. During the nomination process, Frederick received a vote himself. This made him the first African American to be nominated for president of the United States. After Harrison took office in 1889, he appointed

Frederick's grandson Joseph Douglass (1871-1935) was a concert violinist. He often entertained visitors with his beautiful music during their stay at Cedar HIll.

Frederick to be minister resident and consul general to the Republic of Haiti. Frederick was proud to serve his country once again, but during this term of service his loyalty was tested. By the late 1800's, America had become a world power with an impressive military. Haiti, on the other hand, was a small, impoverished nation. The U.S. government had used strong-arm tactics to achieve its goal of establishing a naval base on Haiti's shores. This did not go over well with Frederick. He witnessed the prejudice of American officials who came to the capital of Port-au-Prince to arrange commercial and political deals. Frederick did not like what he saw. He thought highly of the people of Haiti and their elected leaders. Like himself, many of them had once been slaves or were descendants of slaves. The people of Haiti had a high opinion of Frederick as well. In 1892, the Haitian government appointed him as a commissioner of its country's pavilion at the World's Columbian Exposition in Chicago to commemorate the four hundredth anniversary of Columbus's voyage to America. After two years of service as minister resident and consul general, Frederick resigned because of strong disagreements with U.S. policy.

Father of the American Civil Rights Movement

Decades after the Civil War, the United States was still healing its wounds from the terrible conflict. The era of Reconstruction came to an end, and a period of terror and mob violence swept the nation. Incidents of lynching became rampant throughout the South.

White citizens took the law into their own hands and publicly executed African Americans for presumed crimes. Many innocent people lost their lives under the rule of "Lynch Law." Frederick was greatly saddened by this turn of events. To escape this violence, many African Americans, calling themselves "Exodusters," began to move to places on the frontier like Kansas. There they formed all-black communities to enjoy greater freedom and autonomy. Frederick didn't support this, however. He urged African Americans to stay involved in their local communities and not be relegated to the sidelines. African Americans also began to move to large cities in the North. Regrettably, things were little better there. Many people in the North began to believe the lies spread by Southern politicians and others that African Americans did not deserve full citizenship and were ill-prepared to vote. Frederick could see what was happening. The tide of public opinion was turning against the former slaves. Southern sentiment and Northern apathy were working hand in hand to take away African Americans' right to vote. Frederick had fought too long and too hard to let that happen. Now in his 70's, he found a new cause to fight for. Through his countless lectures during those years, Frederick troubled the conscience of America and raised his voice to make the truth heard.

A new generation was rising to challenge the old foes of prejudice, racism, and violence.

Fortunately, he was not alone. A new generation was rising to challenge the old foes of prejudice, racism, and violence. Among them was a young African

American woman named Ida B. Wells (later Wells-Barnett), a tireless journalist from Memphis, Tennessee. Ida exposed the horrible epidemic of lynching that gripped the South during the late 1800's and early 1900's. After a brief correspondence, she and Frederick became friends. The two of them had much in common. Both were editors and orators, and both began their careers fighting the worst form of injustice visited upon the African American community of their respective times. In 1893, they collaborated on a pamphlet about the deceitful and often brutal nature of racism. Ida inspired Frederick. With young people like her, he was certain that the fight for civil rights would continue well after he was gone. And he was right. In 1909, Ida became one of the founding members of the National Association for the Advancement of Colored People (NAACP).

In January 1894, Frederick spoke at the Metropolitan A.M.E. Church in Washington. This address, known as "The Lessons of the Hour," was to be the last great speech of his career. He told his listeners that the so-called and misnamed "Negro Problem" that was sweeping America was nothing of the kind. The difficulties that the country was experiencing were not the fault of its African American citizens. This thinking had to come to an end. The problem was the nation's problem—it was up to everyone to work together to resolve it. "Let the nation try justice," he said, "and the problem will be solved."

Frederick collaborated on a pamphlet about racism with Ida B. Wells-Barnett (1862-1931), a journalist. Wells-Barnett (above) exposed the horrible epidemic of lynching of African Americans that gripped the South during the late 1800's and early 1900's.

On February 20, 1895, days after his 77th birthday, Frederick appeared at a women's rights conference in Washington. Among the attendees was Susan B. Anthony, Frederick's longtime friend and a leader in the woman suffrage movement. Arm in arm, the two great reformers entered the hall to a thunderous round of applause. After the meeting, Frederick, full of enthusiasm, returned home to Cedar Hill for an early dinner with his wife. That evening, as he was telling Helen about the rally, he began to mimic one of his fellow speakers. During this impromptu performance, Frederick rose from his chair but then suddenly fell to the floor. He had suffered a massive heart attack or a stroke. Helen's delight at finding some time to spend with her husband turned to horror. Frederick Douglass, the Lion of Anacostia, was dead.

As the news of Frederick's death spread, the nation went into mourning. Telegrams of condolence poured into Cedar Hill, as newspapers in America and Europe spread the word of his passing. Four days later, a private funeral service was held at Cedar Hill for the family. In the afternoon, the public funeral took place at Metropolitan A.M.E. Church in Washington. Thousands of people filed past the casket holding Frederick's body to pay their last respects. Many important political leaders were in attendance. Susan B. Anthony read a letter composed by Elizabeth Cady Stanton for the service. That evening, Helen and the three remaining Douglass children—Rosetta, Lewis, and Charles—traveled with Frederick's body on the train to New York. (Frederick Junior died three years earlier in 1892 after a lingering illness.) After another church service in Rochester, Frederick was laid to rest in Mount Hope Cemetery, where his wife Anna and daughter were buried. Years later, Helen had a statue of her late husband erected at the site of his home in Rochester. It was the first of many monuments dedicated to him. Before her death in 1903, Frederick's widow converted their home at Cedar Hill into a memorial. Helen carefully preserved many of Frederick's books, papers, and personal possessions. In 1988, Cedar Hill was established as a national historic site by the U.S. National Park Service.

Born into slavery, Frederick Douglass escaped from bondage to become a giant of the 1800's. He invigorated the antislavery movement in both the United States and Great Britain. His passion for justice inspired thousands of people, black and white, to join in the struggle. He was a complex man of amazing courage and remarkable depth. In an age of oratory, his voice was one of the most impressive.

In 2013, Vice President Joseph Biden speaks during a ceremony in which a statue of Frederick Douglass was permanently placed in Emancipation Hall in the United States Capitol to represent the people of the District of Columbia.

It continues to echo throughout the United States to this day.

As a statesman, Frederick championed the cause that everyone was created equal—blacks and whites, men and women—and he worked tirelessly to gain a measure of equality for all people. As a writer, he revealed the harsh truths of American society and called upon his fellow citizens to better themselves. As a social reformer, he spent his life battling racism and discrimination. As an abolitionist, he fought successfully to rid his country of the horrific institution of slavery. Years later, he was demoralized to see injustice return in the form of mob violence and terror.

Yet his labors were effective. Frederick Douglass's brave actions paved the way for the civil rights movement of the 1960's. He was the forerunner to such people as Rosa Parks, Martin Luther King, Jr., and Malcolm X. More than a century before them, Frederick Douglass challenged prejudice and injustice wherever he went. He would sit down in the front sections of trains, streetcars, and steamships that were reserved for whites. Walking into segregated restaurants, he would take a seat and wait to be served. He worked successfully to integrate the public schools in the places he lived. He boycotted any establishment that treated African Americans as second-class citizens. Through a lifetime of battling racism and segregation, Frederick Douglass changed the world and is known today as the "Father of the American Civil Rights Movement."

INDEX

A

abolitionism: in autobiographies, 41-45; of Brown, 56-59; in "Fifth of July" speech, 55; Frederick's first awareness of, 15; of Garrison, 30-32, 36, 68; "Hundred Conventions," 38-40; of Lincoln, 60, 63-66; of Massachusetts Anti-Slavery Society, 35-37; at Nantucket convention, 33-34; of *The North Star,* 50; Zion Church speeches, 32-33

African Americans, 8; in Civil War, 61-63; in Congress, 75; emancipation, 63-66; Frederick on Lincoln and, 77-78; Reconstruction era, 68-70, 87-88

African Methodist Episcopal (A. M. E.) Zion Church, 30-33, 50, 83

American Anti-Slavery Society, 31, 38, 56, 68

Anthony, Aaron, 8, 10-11, 16, 43, 80-81

Anthony, Susan B., 52, 90

antislavery. *See* abolitionism

Auld, Hugh, 12-15, 19-22, 81

Auld, Lucretia, 12, 16, 71

Auld, Sophia, 12-15

Auld, Thomas, 41, 71; Frederick's last meeting with, 80-82; frees Frederick, 47; as slave owner, 12, 16, 17, 19, 71

Auld, Tommy, 14

B

Bailey, Betsey (Betty), 9-11

Bailey, Harriet, 8-10

Bailey, Isaac, 9

Ball, Thomas, 76

Baltimore, 12-16, 19-21, 81, 85

Biden, Joseph, 91

"Bleeding Kansas," 58

Booth, John Wilkes, 66

Boston, Massachusetts, 37, 41, 48, 63-64

Bradburn, George, 39-40

Brown, John, 57-59

C

Cambria, 45, 48

Canada, 18, 26, 49, 58

Catholic Emancipation Act, 46

Cedar Hill, 81-83, 86, 90, 91

civil rights movement, 92

Civil War, U.S., 42, 43, 70, 72, 76, 78, 87; end of, 63-66, 68; events leading to, 53-59; Lincoln and, 59-66

Clarkson, Thomas, 46

Clay, Henry, 54

Coffin, William, 33

Collins, John, 35

Columbian Orator, The, 15, 16, 35

Compromise of 1850, 54

Confederacy, 58, 61-63, 66, 69

Congress, U.S., 15, 63, 76

Constitution, U.S., 50; 13th Amendment, 63; 14th Amendment, 72; 15th Amendment, 72, 73

Cork, Ireland, 46

Covey, Edward, 16-17

D

Douglas, Stephen, 54

Douglass, Anna Murray, 19-22, 37, 59, 69; marriage to Frederick, 26; in New Bedford, 28-30; in Rochester, 49; in Washington, D.C., 82-85

Douglass, Annie, 29, 59

Douglass, Charles Remond, 29, 37, 62, 83, 90-91

Douglass, Frederick: Anna Murray, first meeting with, 19-21; bank venture by, 69; books by, 41-44, 56, 83-84; in British Isles, 44-48, 85-86; civil rights movement and, 92; death, 90-91; on Dred Scott decision, 56; early years, 8-10; education and, 14-15, 18, 40, 55-56; emancipation of, 47; escape to North, 21-26; "Fifth of July" speech, 55; Freedman's Memorial address, 75-78; on Fugitive Slave Act, 54-55; Harpers Ferry raid and, 57-58; at "Hundred Conventions" meetings, 38, 40-41; injury during mob action, 39-40; Lincoln and, 59-66, 69, 76-78; marriages, 26, 84-85; with Massachusetts Anti-Slavery Society, 35-37; at Nantucket convention, 33-35; in New Bedford, 28-33; at New York convention, 39; as newspaper publisher, 48-50, 75; racial justice concerns after Civil War, 68-72, 87-90; reunion with slaveholders, 80-81; as slave, 11-21; as statesman, 72-75, 86-87, 92; women's rights and, 52-53, 72, 90

Douglass, Frederick, Jr., 29, 48, 62-63, 83, 91

Douglass, Joseph, 83, 86

Douglass, Lewis Henry, 29, 48, 62, 63, 71, 83, 90-91

Douglass, Rosetta, 29, 75, 82-83, 90-91

E

East Baltimore Mental Improvement Society, 20

Edinburgh, Scotland, 48

education, 14-15, 18, 40, 55-56

Egypt, 86

Elm Street Methodist Church, 29-30

Emancipation Memorial. *See* Freedman's Memorial

Emancipation Proclamation, 63-65

Enforcement Acts, 73

Equal Rights Party, 74

Exodusters, 88

F

Fells Point, 12-15

"Fifth of July" speech 55

Fort Sumter, 60-61

Fort Wagner, Second Battle of, 63

Frederic Douglass' Paper, 50, 75

Freedman's Memorial, 75-78

Freedman's Savings and Trust Company, 69

Freeland, William, 17-19

Fugitive Slave Act, 54-55

fugitive slave laws, 31, 37-38, 54-55

"Fugitive's Song, The," 34, 35

G

Garfield, James, 43, 73-74, 84

Garnet, Henry Highland, 39

Garrison, William Lloyd, 41, 44, 46; disagreement with Frederick, 46-50, 53, 68; mentor to Frederick, 30-32, 36-39

Grant, Ulysses S., 66, 72-74, 76-77

Great Britain, 21, 45-48, 50, 58-59, 85-86, 91

Griffiths, Julia, 47-48, 50

H

Haiti, 44, 87

Harpers Ferry raid, 56-59

Harrison, Benjamin, 74, 86-87

Hayes, Rutherford B., 73, 80

Hewlett, Virginia, 83

"Hundred Conventions," 38-40

I

Ireland, 46, 85-86

J

Jennings, Thomas and Ann, 46

"Jim Crow" laws, 68, 70

Johnson, Andrew, 69, 71

Johnson, Nathan and Mary, 28

K

King, Martin Luther, Jr., 92

Ku Klux Klan, 70

L

Lady of the Lake, The (Scott), 28

Latimer, George, 37-38

Lee, Robert E., 58, 66

Liberator, The, 30-32, 36

Liberty Party, 56

Life and Times of Frederick Douglass (Douglass), 42, 83-84

Lincoln, Abraham, 43, 69; Civil War and, 59-66; Frederick on, 77-78; monument to, 76-77

Liverpool, England, 45-46

Lloyd, Edward, 10, 11, 81-82

Lloyd, Howard, 82

Loguen, Helen, 83

Louverture, Toussaint, 44

lynching, 87-89

Lynn, Massachusetts, 36

M

Malcolm X, 92

Mason-Dixon Line, 18

Massachusetts, 37-38, 44, 49

Massachusetts Anti-Slavery

Society, 35-37

May, Samuel J., 37

Metropolitan African
Methodist Episcopal (A.
M. E.), 89, 90

Mexico, 53-54

Mott, Lucretia, 52

Murray, Anna. *See* Douglass,
Anna Murray

My Bondage and My Freedom
(Douglass), 42-43, 56

N

Nantucket Anti-Slavery
Convention, 33-35

*Narrative of the Life of
Frederick Douglass:
An American Slave*
(Douglass), 41-42

National Association for the
Advancement of Colored
People (NAACP), 89

National Convention of
Colored Citizens, 39

National Union Convention,
71

New Bedford, Massachusetts,
28-30, 33, 36

New York, 38, 39, 91. *See also*
Rochester, New York

New York City, 22, 25-26, 30

New York Vigilance
Committee, 26

North Star, The, 48-50, 52,
53, 75

O

O'Connell, Daniel, 46

"Old Master." *See* Anthony,
Aaron

P

Parks, Rosa, 92

Pendleton, Indiana, 39-40

Pennington, James W. C., 26

Philadelphia, 25, 56-57, 71-72

Phillips, Wendell, 37

Pitts, Helen, 84-86, 90-91

Port-au-Prince, Haiti, 87

R

Radical Republicans, 69

reading, 14-15, 18

Reconstruction, 68-70, 87

Remond, Charles Lenox,
37-39

Republican Party, 59, 60, 69,
86

Richardson, Anna, 47

Richardson, Ellen, 47

Rochester, New York, 54-
55, 58, 59, 66, 71, 80, 82;
destruction of Douglass
home, 75; monument, 91;
move to, 49-50

Rochester Ladies' Anti-
Slavery Society, 55

Ruggles, David, 25-26, 28

Rush, Christopher, 30

S

St. Michaels, Maryland, 16-
19

Scott, Dred, 56

Sears, Amanda Auld, 71-72

segregation, 29-30, 68, 70

Seneca Falls Convention,
52-53

slavery, Frederick's first
awareness of, 10-11. *See
also* abolitionism

Smith, Gerrit, 50

Sprague, Nathan, 82

Stanton, Elizabeth Cady, 52-
53, 72, 85, 90

Stuart (sailor), 25

suffrage: African American,
65-66, 70-73, 88; women's,
72, 90

Supreme Court, U.S., 56, 76

T

Talbot County, Maryland,
8-12, 19, 80

Truth, Sojourner, 30

Tubman, Harriet, 30

U

underground railroad, 24,
26, 28, 49, 53-55

United States Colored Troops
(USCT), 62-64

V

voting. *See* suffrage

W

Washington, D.C., 64, 66,
71; Freedman's Memorial,
75-78; later years in, 80-87,
89, 90

Wells-Barnett, Ida B., 89

West Indies, 44-45, 50

White, William A., 39-40

Wilmington, Delaware, 23-
25

women's rights, 52-53, 72, 90

Woodhull, Victoria, 74

World's Columbian
Exposition, 87

Wye House Plantation, 10-
12, 15, 82

FURTHER READING

Bolden, Tonya. *Facing Frederick: The Life of Frederick Douglass.* Abrams Bks. for Young Readers, 2017.

Frederick Douglass National Historic Site. https://www.nps.gov/frdo/index.htm

Frederick Douglass Papers at the Library of Congress. https://www.loc.gov /collections/frederick-douglass-papers/

Thompson, Mary J., and others, eds. *The Frederick Douglass Encyclopedia.* Greenwood, 2009.

ACKNOWLEDGMENTS

Cover: Mathew B. Brady, Gilman Collection/Metropolitan Museum of Art

3 © Everett Historical/Shutterstock	61 Library of Congress
7-9 © Duncan1890/iStockphoto	62 Smithsonian National Museum of African American History and Culture
10 Library of Congress	
13 © The Print Collector/Getty Images	
15 Library of Congress	65-68 Library of Congress
16 Public Domain	73 © Everett HistoricalShutterstock
20 Library of Congress	74 Smithsonian National Museum of African American History and Culture
23 © Fotosearch/Getty Images	
24-27 Library of Congress	
29 © Universal History Archive/ Getty Images	76 © Valerii Iavtushenko, Shutterstock
	79 © Shutterstock
31-34 Library of Congress	81 Jack Rottier, National Park Service
37 © Everett Historical/Shutterstock	82 © Everett Historical/Shutterstock
40 Library of Congress	85 National Park Service
42 Public Domain	86 Library of Congress
47 © Bettmann/Getty Images	89 Public Domain
49-51 Library of Congress	91 © Linda Davidson, The Washington Post/Getty Images
52-54 Public Domain	
57 © Everett Historical/Shutterstock	